The No Code SaaS Millionaire

By Daniel Melehi

© January 18th 2024

# Contents

Introduction...................................................................17

*Chapter 1: The Rise of No Code* ....................................18

The Origins of No Code.............................................18

The Need for No Code ..............................................19

The Advantages of No Code .....................................19

    1. Accessibility: ...................................................19

    2. Speed and Efficiency: ......................................20

    3. Cost-Effectiveness: ..........................................20

    4. Flexibility and Iteration:...................................20

The Growing Popularity of No Code .........................21

What is SAAS?...........................................................22

    Features of SAAS .................................................22

    Benefits of SAAS .................................................23

    SAAS Business Models..........................................23

*Chapter 3: Benefits of No Code SAAS* ...........................24

1. Accessibility........................................................25

2. Speed and Efficiency............................................25

3. Cost-effectiveness ..............................................25

4. Flexibility............................................................26

5. Seamless Collaboration .......................................26

*Chapter 5: Introduction to ChatGPT* ............................27

Understanding ChatGPT ...........................................28

The Benefits of ChatGPT in SAAS..............................28

Integrating ChatGPT in SAAS Applications ...................29

*Chapter 6: How ChatGPT Works with SAAS*...................**32**

Understanding ChatGPT ...................................**32**

Benefits of Integrating ChatGPT with SAAS ...................**33**
  1. Enhanced Customer Support.............................33
  2. Improved User Engagement.............................33
  3. Time and Cost Savings ....................................34
  4. Scalability.....................................................34
  5. Data Collection and Analysis ...........................34

Integrating ChatGPT with SAAS ...................**35**

Conclusion ...................................................**35**

*Chapter 7: Integrating ChatGPT in SAAS Applications* ..**36**

Understanding ChatGPT ...................................**36**

Benefits of Integrating ChatGPT with SAAS ...................**37**
  Enhanced Customer Support ..............................37
  Improved User Engagement................................37
  Time and Cost Savings .......................................37
  Scalability ......................................................38
  Data Collection and Analysis ...............................38

Integrating ChatGPT with SAAS Applications ...............**38**
  Step 1: Setting Up the API ...................................38
  Step 2: Defining Use Cases .................................39
  Step 3: Designing Chat Interfaces.........................39
  Step 4: Implementing ChatGPT API Calls................39
  Step 5: Context Management and Error Handling ...............39
  Step 6: User Feedback and Iterative Improvement..............40

Conclusion ...................................................**40**

*Chapter 8: Building Your First No Code SAAS Application*
.......................................................................................*40*

1. Define Your Application's Purpose and Target Audience
.......................................................................................41

2. Research No Code Platforms .......................................41

3. Select the Right Tools and Components......................42

4. Design Your Application's User Interface ...................42

5. Customize and Configure Functionality......................42

6. Test and Iterate .........................................................43

7. Deploy and Launch Your SAAS Application ................43

8. Continue to Improve and Scale...................................44

Conclusion ....................................................................44

*Chapter 9: Monetizing Your SAAS Application.............44*

1. Subscription Model ....................................................45

2. Usage-Based Pricing ...................................................45

3. Freemium....................................................................46

4. One-Time Purchase ....................................................46

5. Add-Ons and Upsells ..................................................47

6. Partner Programs .......................................................47

    Conclusion .........................................................................47

*Chapter 10: Pricing Models for SAAS Applications........48*

1. Subscription Model ....................................................48

2. Usage-Based Pricing ...................................................49

4

3. Freemium Model.................................................50

4. One-Time Purchase Model ...............................50

5. Add-Ons and Upsells ......................................51

6. Partner Programs/Reseller Agreements ...............52

*Chapter 11: Marketing Your No Code SAAS Application*
.......................................................................*53*

1. Define Your Target Audience ...........................53

2. Develop a Compelling Value Proposition .............54

3. Create an Engaging Website ............................54

4. Content Marketing .......................................55

5. Social Media Marketing...................................55

6. Influencer Marketing......................................55

7. Referral Programs .........................................56

8. User Reviews and Testimonials .........................56

9. Email Marketing ..........................................57

10. Analyze and Refine Your Marketing Efforts..............57

*Chapter 12: Growing Your User Base* ...............*58*

1. User Acquisition Strategies...............................58

   a. Content Marketing ...............................................58
   b. Social Media Marketing..........................................59
   c. Influencer Marketing .............................................59
   d. Referral Programs ................................................59
   e. Search Engine Optimization (SEO).........................59

2. User Engagement and Retention .......................60

a. Personalization and Customization ....................................60

b. Regular Updates and Enhancements ...............................60

c. Proactive Customer Support............................................61

d. Gamification ..................................................................61

**3. User Feedback and Iterative Improvement.................61**

**4. Partnership and Collaborations ..................................61**

**Conclusion ...................................................................62**

***Chapter 13: Retaining Customers for Long-Term Success***
***...............................................................................62***

**The Importance of Customer Retention .........................62**

**Strategies for Customer Retention ................................63**

1. Offer Exceptional Customer Support ...............................63

2. Provide Regular Updates and Enhancements ...................63

3. Personalization and Customization ..................................64

4. Proactive Customer Outreach .........................................64

5. Loyalty Programs and Rewards .......................................64

**Monitoring Customer Retention Metrics.........................65**

**In Summary...................................................................65**

***Chapter 14: Scaling Your SAAS Business.........................66***

**The Importance of Scaling .............................................66**

**Strategies for Scaling Your SAAS Business .......................67**

**Measuring and Monitoring Scaling Success .....................68**

**Conclusion ...................................................................69**

***Chapter 15: Lessons from Successful No Code SAAS***
***Entrepreneurs...............................................................70***

Introduction ...................................................70

Lesson 1: Start with a Problem .........................70

Lesson 2: Build Simple and Intuitive Applications ..........71

Lesson 3: Embrace Continuous Improvement ................71

Lesson 4: Focus on Customer Success ...........................72

Lesson 5: Develop a Strong Brand and Marketing Strategy
...................................................................73

Conclusion ...................................................73

*Chapter 17: Leveraging Automation in No Code SAAS..74*

Understanding Automation in No Code SAAS .................74
The Benefits of Automation ..................................75

Implementing Automation in No Code SAAS ..................75

The Future of Automation in No Code SAAS ..................76
Conclusion ..................................................77

*Chapter 17: Leveraging Automation in No Code SAAS..77*

The Benefits of Automation ..............................78
1. Improved Efficiency....................................78
2. Cost Savings.........................................78
3. Increased Productivity.................................78
4. Enhanced Accuracy ..................................79
5. Scalability...........................................79

Strategies for Implementing Automation ......................79
1. Identify Areas for Automation...........................79
2. Choose the Right Automation Tools......................80
3. Streamline Workflows .................................80
4. Implement Automation Gradually ......................80

5. Continuously Monitor and Improve ....................................80

**The Future of Automation in No Code SAAS** ...................81

**Leveraging Automation for Success** ...............................82

*Chapter 18: Innovating and Staying Ahead in the No Code SAAS Industry* .......................................................82

**Innovating in the No Code SAAS Industry** ......................83

**Staying Ahead in the No Code SAAS Industry** ................84

*Chapter 19: Building a Team for Your SAAS Business* ...85

**The Importance of a Strong Team** .................................86

**Building Your SAAS Team** ............................................86

Identify Roles and Responsibilities .......................................87

Define Desired Skills and Qualifications ...............................87

Recruitment and Hiring ......................................................87

Training and Development ...................................................88

Team Collaboration and Communication .............................88

Retention and Recognition ..................................................88

**Conclusion** .................................................................89

*Chapter 20: Outsourcing and Freelancing in the No Code SAAS Space* ..................................................................89

**The Advantages of Outsourcing and Freelancing** ...........90

Access to Global Talent .......................................................90

Cost-Effectiveness ..............................................................90

Flexibility and Scalability .....................................................91

Focus on Core Competencies ...............................................91

**Considerations for Outsourcing and Freelancing** ...........91

Clear Communication and Expectations ................................92

Quality Assurance and Management .....................................92

Data Security and Confidentiality............................................92

Managing Multiple Vendors or Freelancers.........................93

**Conclusion** ....................................................................**93**

***Chapter 21: Legal Considerations for Your SAAS Business***
..................................................................................***94***

**Understanding Intellectual Property Rights..................94**

Trademark Registration......................................................94

Copyright Protection ..........................................................95

Software Licensing ..............................................................95

**Data Privacy and Security..............................................95**

Privacy Policies ...................................................................96

Data Transfer and Storage..................................................96

User Consent and Opt-Out Mechanisms.............................96

**Contractual Agreements and Terms of Service ..............96**

Terms of Service .................................................................97

Service Level Agreements (SLAs)........................................97

Vendor and Partner Agreements .......................................97

**Compliance with Industry Regulations ..........................97**

Health Insurance Portability and Accountability Act (HIPAA)
.............................................................................................98

Payment Card Industry Data Security Standard (PCI DSS)....98

Financial Regulations..........................................................98

**Conclusion** ....................................................................**98**

***Chapter 22: Customer Support and Success Strategies .99***

**The Importance of Customer Support and Success ........99**

**Strategies for Effective Customer Support and Success.100**

1. Proactive Support..........................................................100

2. Prompt and Responsive Communication ......................101

3. Personalization and Customization ...................................101

4. Customer Onboarding and Training ..............................101

5. Continuous Education and Engagement .......................102

6. Customer Success Managers...........................................102

7. Gather and Act on Customer Feedback.........................102

8. Measure Customer Success Metrics...............................103

**Conclusion** .................................................................**103**

**Chapter 23: Analyzing Data for Improved SAAS Performance**...............................................................**103**

**The Importance of Data Analysis** ...................................**104**

1. Understanding User Behavior: ........................................104

2. Identifying Bottlenecks and Performance Issues: ..........104

3. Personalization and Customization: ................................105

4. Decision-making and Strategic Planning: ......................105

**Strategies for Leveraging Data Analysis** ........................**105**

1. Define Key Performance Metrics: ...................................106

2. Implement Analytics Tools: ............................................106

3. Utilize Data Visualization Techniques:............................106

4. Conduct A/B Testing:.......................................................107

5. Continuously Monitor and Iteratively Improve: .............107

**Conclusion** .................................................................**107**

**Chapter 24: The Role of UX/UI Design in No Code SAAS** ...............................................................................**108**

**The Importance of UX/UI Design in No Code SAAS** .......**108**

**Best Practices for UX/UI Design in No Code SAAS** .........**109**

**Conclusion** .................................................................**111**

**Chapter 25: Developing API Integrations for Your SAAS Application** .................................................................**111**

**Understanding API Integration** .......................................112

**Benefits of API Integrations** .........................................112

    Expanded Functionality: ...........................................112

    Improved User Experience: ......................................113

    Streamlined Workflows: ...........................................113

    Scalability and Flexibility: .........................................113

    Competitive Advantage: ...........................................113

**Developing API Integrations** ........................................114

    Identify Integration Opportunities: ......................114

    Understand API Documentation: .........................114

    Plan Integration Workflow: ....................................114

    Develop Integration Code: .....................................115

    Test and Debug: .........................................................115

    Document Integration: .............................................115

    Monitor and Maintain: .............................................115

**Conclusion** ..................................................................116

*Chapter 26: Securing Your SAAS Application and User Data* .............................................................................116

**Importance of Securing Your SAAS Application and User Data** ...................................................................116

**Understanding the Risks** ............................................117

**Implementing Security Measures** ...........................117

**Compliance and Regulations** ....................................119

**Conclusion** ..................................................................119

*Chapter 28: Case Study: From No Code to SAAS Millionaire* .....................................................................120

**Case Study: John's Entrepreneurial Journey** ..........120

Key Takeaways .................................................................122

*Chapter 29: Tips for Building a Profitable SAAS
Marketplace* ...................................................................*123*

   **1. Identify a Niche Market** ...........................................**123**

   **2. Build a User-Friendly Interface** ...............................**124**

   **3. Implement Secure Payment Systems** ......................**124**

   **4. Provide Efficient Customer Support** .......................**125**

   **5. Implement Effective Marketing Strategies** ...............**125**

   **6. Foster Trust and Safety** ..........................................**125**

   **7. Encourage User Engagement** ..................................**126**

   **8. Continuously Improve and Innovate** .......................**126**

*Chapter 30: Building Custom Extensions for SAAS
Applications* ...................................................................*127*

   **Understanding the Importance of Custom Extensions** ..**127**

   **The Benefits of Building Custom Extensions** ................**128**

   **Building Custom Extensions for SAAS Applications** .......**129**

   **Conclusion** ................................................................**130**

*Chapter 31: Leveraging Analytics to Drive Revenue....130*

   **Understanding the Importance of Analytics** ................**131**

     1. Customer Behavior Analysis: ...........................131

     2. Identify Revenue Opportunities: ......................131

     3. Optimize Pricing and Packaging: ......................132

     4. Churn Prediction and Reduction: ......................132

     5. Performance and Optimization: ........................132

**Strategies for Leveraging Analytics to Drive Revenue ...133**

1. Define Key Performance Indicators (KPIs):......................133
2. Utilize Advanced Analytics Tools: ...................................133
3. Implement A/B Testing:....................................................134
4. Personalization and Upselling: ........................................134
5. Cohort Analysis and Customer Segmentation:...............134
6. Predictive Analytics: .......................................................134
7. Implement Data-Driven Decision-Making: .....................135

**In Conclusion................................................................135**

***Chapter 32: The Future of No Code SAAS....................135***

**Rise of AI and Automation...........................................136**

**Integration with Emerging Technologies.......................136**

**Enhanced Collaboration and Co-Creation .....................137**

**Advanced Customization and Personalization .............138**

**The Evolving Role of No Code Developers....................138**

**Conclusion .................................................................139**

**Chapter 33: Personal Branding and Thought Leadership in the SAAS Space .........................................................139**

The Power of Personal Branding .........................................140
Developing Thought Leadership...........................................141
Benefits of Personal Branding and Thought Leadership in SAAS ...................................................................................142
Conclusion ...........................................................................143

***Chapter 34: Mental Strategies for Success as a SAAS Entrepreneur .............................................................143***

**1. Embrace a Growth Mindset .....................................143**

**2. Stay Resilient..........................................................144**

**3. Foster a Problem-Solving Attitude** ...........................145

**4. Cultivate Strong Communication Skills** ....................145

**5. Maintain a Positive and Persistent Attitude**.............146

**Conclusion** ................................................................146

***Chapter 35: Nurturing Partnerships and Collaborations***
..................................................................................***147***

**The Power of Partnerships** ...........................................147

**Strategies for Nurturing Partnerships and Collaborations**
..................................................................................148

**Conclusion** ................................................................149

***Chapter 36: Building SAAS for Niche Markets***.............***150***

**Why Target Niche Markets in SAAS?** ...........................150
    Limited Competition:...............................................150
    Higher Profit Margins: .............................................151
    Enhanced Customer Satisfaction:...........................151
    Word-of-Mouth Marketing: .....................................151
    Opportunity for Expansion:......................................151

**Identifying Your Niche Market** .....................................152
    Market Research: .....................................................152
    Customer Persona Development: ............................152
    Competitive Analysis:...............................................152
    Validation: ...............................................................153
    Scalability: ...............................................................153

**Tailoring Your SAAS Application to the Niche Market**...153
    Customization and Personalization:.......................154
    Industry-specific Features: ......................................154
    Domain Expertise: ...................................................154

Seamless Integration: ............................................154

Continuous Feedback Loop: ...............................155

**Conclusion** ...............................................**155**

***Chapter 37: Overcoming Imposter Syndrome in the SAAS Industry*** .....................................................***155***

**Understanding Imposter Syndrome**...........................**156**

**The Impact of Imposter Syndrome in the SAAS Industry** .........................................................**156**

**Strategies for Overcoming Imposter Syndrome** ..........**157**

**Conclusion** ...............................................**158**

***Chapter 38: Earning Passive Income with No Code SAAS*** .....................................................***158***

**Understanding Passive Income**...............................**159**

**Monetizing Your No Code SAAS Application** ...............**159**

Subscription Model ...........................................159

License Fees.................................................160

Upselling and Add-Ons .......................................160

Affiliate Partnerships.........................................160

White Labeling and Reseller Programs...............161

Advertising and Sponsorships .............................161

Marketplace Revenue ......................................161

**Automating Business Operations** ..........................**162**

User Onboarding and Support ...........................162

Payment Processing and Invoicing ......................162

Analytics and Reporting ....................................163

Marketing and Lead Generation .........................163

Infrastructure Scaling and Maintenance ..............163

Conclusion ..................................................................164

*Chapter 40: Becoming a Millionaire with No Code SAAS*
*Applications...............................................................166*

Identify a Problem and Market Demand.......................167

Create a Compelling Value Proposition........................167

Build a User-Friendly and Intuitive SAAS Application....167

Implement Effective Monetization Strategies...............168

Execute a Comprehensive Marketing Strategy.............168

Focus on Customer Success and Retention ..................169

Continuously Innovate and Scale.................................169

Stay Resilient and Persist ..........................................170

Conclusion ........................................................170

# Introduction

Welcome to "The No Code SaaS Millionaire" – a comprehensive guide to building successful Software as a Service (SaaS) applications without coding. This book is designed to provide aspiring entrepreneurs, developers, and business enthusiasts with the knowledge and tools needed to create and scale their own SaaS businesses using no-code platforms. In recent years, the rise of no-code and low-code development tools has revolutionized the software industry. No longer do you need to be a skilled programmer to create sophisticated web and mobile applications. No-code platforms empower individuals with diverse skill sets and backgrounds to turn their innovative ideas into reality. Throughout this book, we will explore the various aspects of building a SaaS business without writing a single line of code. You will discover the potential of no-code platforms, the benefits they offer, and how they can be leveraged to create scalable and profitable SaaS applications. Chapter by chapter, we will delve into the fundamentals of SaaS and explore real-world examples of successful no-code SaaS companies. We will also discuss the integration of advanced language models like ChatGPT in SaaS applications, and how to monetize, market, and grow your user base. You will learn about common challenges faced by no-code SaaS entrepreneurs and discover strategies to overcome them. We will cover topics such as leveraging automation, staying ahead in the industry, building effective teams, and managing customer support. Understanding the legal considerations, data analysis, UX/UI design, API integrations, and security protocols will also be explored in detail. Additionally, we will delve into the future prospects of no-code SaaS, personal branding, mental strategies for success, passive income generation, and even investing in startups within the industry. By the end of this book, you will have a strong understanding of how to build, scale, and monetize your own no-code SaaS application, and potentially find yourself on the path to becoming a SaaS millionaire. So, let's embark on this exciting journey and uncover the world of no-code SaaS entrepreneurship. Let's get started on your path to becoming a No Code SaaS Millionaire!

# Chapter 1: The Rise of No Code

No code development has gained significant traction in recent years, revolutionizing the way software applications are built and empowering individuals without technical expertise to create their own digital solutions. This chapter explores the rise of the no code movement, its origins, and the factors that have contributed to its popularity.

## THE ORIGINS OF NO CODE

Traditionally, developing software applications required extensive coding knowledge and expertise, often limiting the ability to create digital solutions to a select few. However, with advancements in technology and the increasing demand for user-friendly tools, the concept of no code emerged as a solution to democratize the software development process. No code ideologies can be traced back to the early days of visual programming languages, such as Scratch and Alice, which allowed individuals to create programs using visual blocks instead of writing lines of code. These platforms sparked the idea that coding knowledge should not be a prerequisite for creating digital solutions.

# THE NEED FOR NO CODE

The demand for software applications has skyrocketed in recent years, as businesses and individuals recognize the benefits of automation, digitization, and streamlined processes. However, the shortage of skilled developers and the time required to learn complex coding languages have created a bottleneck in meeting this demand. No code platforms emerged as a response to these challenges, offering a simplified approach to application development. By using intuitive interfaces and drag-and-drop functionality, no code tools enable users to visually create applications without writing a single line of code.

# THE ADVANTAGES OF NO CODE

The rise of no code has brought numerous advantages to the world of application development. Some of the key benefits include:

# 1. Accessibility:

No code platforms break down the barriers to entry, allowing individuals from various backgrounds to participate in software development. This accessibility has opened up new opportunities for entrepreneurs, small businesses, and non-technical professionals to bring their ideas to life.

# 2. Speed and Efficiency:

No code tools significantly reduce the time and effort required to create software applications. With pre-built modules and integrations, users can leverage existing functionalities, eliminating the need to start from scratch. This speeds up the development process and enables rapid prototyping.

# 3. Cost-Effectiveness:

Traditional software development often comes with hefty price tags, requiring substantial investment in hiring skilled developers or outsourcing the project. In contrast, no code solutions are more cost-effective, as they eliminate the need for coding expertise, allowing businesses to allocate their resources more efficiently.

# 4. Flexibility and Iteration:

No code platforms embrace an iterative approach to application development, allowing users to quickly make changes and updates to their software. This flexibility enables businesses to adapt to evolving market demands and user feedback, ultimately leading to better products and user experiences.

# THE GROWING POPULARITY OF NO CODE

The rise of no code has been fueled by several factors, including the proliferation of SaaS (Software as a Service) models, advancements in cloud computing, and the demand for agile software development. SaaS platforms have played a significant role in popularizing no code, as many of these platforms offer built-in no code tools that allow users to create customizations and integrations without the need for coding skills. This accessibility has empowered businesses and individuals to tailor software applications to their specific needs. Furthermore, the scalability and cost-effectiveness of cloud computing have made it easier for no code platforms to operate and deliver exceptional user experiences. The cloud provides the necessary infrastructure to host, scale, and maintain applications created using no code tools. Agile software development methodologies have also contributed to the rise of no code. The iterative nature of no code development aligns perfectly with the agile principles of collaboration, flexibility, and continuous improvement. Overall, the rise of no code has transformed the software development landscape, democratizing the process and empowering a new generation of digital creators. In the following chapters, we will explore the potential of no code SaaS (Software as a Service) and how it can pave the way for aspiring entrepreneurs to build profitable businesses without any coding experience.Understanding

SAAS SaaS, or Software as a Service, is a software delivery model that has gained immense popularity in recent years. In this chapter, we will dive deep into the concept of SAAS and explore its features, benefits, and business models. Understanding SAAS is crucial for anyone looking to build a successful no code SAAS application and become a millionaire in the industry.

# WHAT IS SAAS?

SAAS is a cloud computing model where software applications are hosted by a service provider and made available to customers over the internet. Instead of purchasing software licenses and installing them on individual machines, users can access the software through a web browser, paying a subscription fee for its usage.

# Features of SAAS

SAAS offers several unique features that distinguish it from traditional software delivery models: 1. Multi-tenant Architecture: SAAS applications are designed to serve multiple customers (tenants) from a single codebase and infrastructure. This ensures cost-effectiveness, scalability, and easier maintenance for the service provider. 2. Automatic Updates: With SAAS, the responsibility of software updates and patches lies with the service provider. Customers automatically receive updates without the need for manual installations, ensuring they always have access to the latest features and security enhancements. 3. Accessibility: SAAS applications are accessible from any device with an internet connection, allowing users to work remotely and collaborate effortlessly. This flexibility is particularly beneficial in today's digital age where remote work is becoming more prevalent. 4. Scalability: SAAS applications can easily scale to accommodate the growing needs of businesses. Service providers can allocate resources based on demand, ensuring optimal performance even during peak usage periods.

# Benefits of SAAS

SAAS offers a range of benefits for both businesses and end-users: 1. Cost-Effectiveness: SAAS eliminates the need for upfront investments in hardware and software licenses, making it a cost-effective solution for businesses. Users pay a subscription fee based on usage, which is often more affordable than purchasing and maintaining software individually. 2. Time and Efficiency: SAAS applications are readily available over the internet, eliminating the time-consuming processes of installation, updates, and maintenance. Users can start using the software immediately, saving time and boosting productivity. 3. Scalability and Flexibility: SAAS allows businesses to easily scale their software resources based on evolving requirements. Whether it's adding more users, integrating new features, or expanding to serve a larger customer base, SAAS offers the flexibility to adapt and grow. 4. Seamless Collaboration: SAAS applications promote collaboration by allowing users to access and work on the same software in real-time. This improves communication, boosts efficiency, and streamlines teamwork, particularly in distributed work environments.

# SAAS Business Models

SAAS companies typically operate under different business models to monetize their software offerings. Some common SAAS business models include: 1. Subscription Model: Under this model, customers pay a recurring subscription fee to access and use the SAAS application. Subscription models can be further categorized into tiers based on features, usage levels, or user roles, allowing customers to choose the plan that best fits their needs. 2. Pay-per-Use Model: In this model, customers are charged based on their actual usage of the SAAS application. Metrics such as resources consumed, number of users, or volume of data processed determine the pricing. This model is particularly suitable for applications with variable usage patterns. 3. Freemium Model: Freemium models offer a basic version of the SAAS application for free, enticing users to upgrade to a paid plan for access to advanced features or increased usage limits. This model allows businesses to attract a wider user base and convert free users into paying customers. Understanding the features, benefits, and business models of SAAS is essential for leveraging the power of no code development in building successful SAAS applications. In the following chapters, we will explore specific strategies and techniques to excel in the no code SAAS industry and achieve millionaire status. But first, let's delve into the benefits of no code SAAS in Chapter 3.

# Chapter 3: Benefits of No Code SAAS

No code software development has proven to be a game-changer for the tech industry, empowering individuals and businesses to create powerful applications without the need for complex coding. When combined with the Software as a Service (SAAS) model, the benefits become even more pronounced. In this chapter, we will explore the advantages that no code SAAS offers and why it has become such a popular choice for entrepreneurs and businesses alike.

## 1. ACCESSIBILITY

One of the key benefits of no code SAAS is its accessibility. Traditional coding can be intimidating and often requires specialized technical skills. However, with the visual interface and drag-and-drop functionalities of no code platforms, even individuals with little to no coding experience can create sophisticated applications. This opens up opportunities for non-technical entrepreneurs and small businesses to enter the software market and bring their ideas to life.

## 2. SPEED AND EFFICIENCY

No code SAAS significantly accelerates the development process by eliminating the need for manual coding. With pre-built templates, customizable components, and a vast library of ready-to-use functionalities, developers can rapidly prototype and deploy applications. This speed not only reduces time to market but also allows for quick iterations and updates as customer feedback and market demands evolve. It enables businesses to stay ahead of the competition and seize opportunities in a fast-paced digital landscape.

# 3. COST-EFFECTIVENESS

Traditional software development can be expensive, requiring skilled developers, infrastructure, and ongoing maintenance costs. No code SAAS, on the other hand, offers a cost-effective alternative. By removing the need for extensive coding and technical expertise, businesses can save considerably on development and staffing costs. Additionally, SAAS models provide subscription-based pricing, eliminating the upfront investment of purchasing individual software licenses. This pay-as-you-go model allows businesses to scale their usage and costs according to their needs, making it particularly attractive for startups and small businesses with limited budgets.

# 4. FLEXIBILITY

No code SAAS platforms offer a high degree of flexibility, enabling users to customize and adapt applications to meet their specific requirements. With a wide range of pre-built templates and modules, developers can easily add or remove functionalities, change layouts, and tailor the user interface without writing a single line of code. This flexibility allows businesses to create applications that align with their unique branding, workflows, and user experience, ultimately delivering a more personalized and engaging product to their customers.

# 5. SEAMLESS COLLABORATION

Collaboration is essential in today's dynamic business environment. No code SAAS applications provide a centralized platform where teams can collaborate and work together efficiently. Since these applications are hosted in the cloud, team members can access and work on projects from anywhere, using any device with an internet connection. Real-time collaboration features, such as shared editing and instant updates, enhance productivity and streamline communication among team members. This collaborative nature of no code SAAS fosters creativity, accelerates decision-making processes, and promotes teamwork. Overall, the benefits of no code SAAS are undeniable. It democratizes software development, making it accessible to a wider audience, accelerates the development process, reduces costs, offers flexibility, and enables seamless collaboration. Whether you are a solopreneur, a small business, or even a large enterprise, no code SAAS can be a powerful tool in your journey to success. In the following chapters, we will delve deeper into specific aspects of no code SAAS and explore how you can leverage these benefits to build and grow your own SAAS business.

# Chapter 5: Introduction to ChatGPT

Chatbots have gained significant popularity in recent years, revolutionizing the way businesses interact with their customers. They provide instant and personalized support, enhance customer experience, and reduce manual workload. One of the key advancements in chatbot technology is the emergence of ChatGPT. ChatGPT is an AI-powered language model developed by OpenAI. It leverages cutting-edge machine learning techniques to generate human-like responses in conversational contexts. With its ability to understand and generate natural language, ChatGPT has become a game-changer in the world of customer support and communication.

## UNDERSTANDING CHATGPT

ChatGPT is built upon the GPT (Generative Pre-trained Transformer) architecture, which is known for its state-of-the-art performance in tasks related to language understanding and generation. The model is trained on a vast amount of text data from the internet, absorbing a wide range of knowledge and linguistic patterns. Unlike traditional rule-based chatbots, ChatGPT relies on machine learning algorithms to learn from data and generate responses. It can process and understand complex queries, provide relevant information, and engage in meaningful conversations with users.

# THE BENEFITS OF CHATGPT IN SAAS

Integrating ChatGPT into SAAS applications can unlock a myriad of benefits for both businesses and customers. Here are some advantages of incorporating ChatGPT in your SAAS product: 1. Enhanced Customer Support: ChatGPT can provide instant and personalized support to customers, answering their queries, resolving issues, and guiding them through complex workflows. This reduces the need for manual intervention, saving time and resources. 2. Improved User Engagement: By leveraging ChatGPT's conversational abilities, SAAS applications can offer a more interactive and engaging user experience. Conversations with the chatbot can feel natural and lifelike, boosting user satisfaction and retention. 3. Time and Cost Savings: ChatGPT can automate repetitive tasks and handle common customer inquiries, freeing up valuable time for customer support teams to focus on more complex issues. This not only improves efficiency but also reduces operational costs. 4. Scalability: As SAAS businesses grow, the demand for customer support also increases. ChatGPT excels in scalability, effortlessly handling multiple conversations simultaneously without compromising performance. 5. Data Collection and Analysis: ChatGPT can gather valuable insights from user interactions, helping businesses understand their customers' needs, preferences, and pain points. The data collected can be further utilized for product improvement and decision-making.

# INTEGRATING CHATGPT IN SAAS APPLICATIONS

To integrate ChatGPT into your SAAS application, you can leverage OpenAI's API, which allows developers to easily interact with the language model. The API enables your application to send user queries to ChatGPT and receive responses in real-time. When integrating ChatGPT, it is important to consider the following: 1. Context Management: ChatGPT performs best when given appropriate context. Ensure that user queries are clear and concise, providing sufficient information for the chatbot to generate accurate responses. 2. Error Handling: As with any AI model, ChatGPT may occasionally produce incorrect or nonsensical answers. Implement error-handling mechanisms to gracefully handle such situations and provide alternate solutions if needed. 3. User Feedback: Encourage users to provide feedback on the chatbot's responses. Collecting user feedback can help improve the accuracy and effectiveness of the chatbot over time. Overall, the introduction of ChatGPT brings tremendous potential for businesses to enhance their SAAS applications with advanced conversational capabilities. From customer support to user engagement, the integration of ChatGPT can significantly elevate the user experience and drive the success of SAAS businesses.# Chapter 5: Introduction to ChatGPT ChatGPT, developed by OpenAI, is an advanced AI-powered language model that has gained significant popularity in recent years. This chapter serves as an introduction to ChatGPT, providing insights into its capabilities and how it can be integrated into SAAS applications. ## What is ChatGPT? ChatGPT is a powerful language model that has been designed to understand and generate natural language responses. It has been trained on a vast amount of text data from the internet, enabling it to mimic human-like conversation. With the ability to understand context and generate relevant responses, ChatGPT has become a valuable tool in various applications, especially in customer support and engagement. ## Benefits of ChatGPT Integration Integrating ChatGPT into SAAS applications offers numerous benefits and can significantly enhance the user experience. Here are some key advantages to consider: 1. **Enhanced Customer Support**: By incorporating ChatGPT, SAAS applications can provide users with instant and personalized support, ensuring their queries are addressed promptly. ChatGPT can understand complex questions and provide accurate responses, resulting in improved customer satisfaction. 2. **Improved User Engagement**: ChatGPT enables interactive conversations with users, enhancing engagement and making interactions more meaningful. Users can easily communicate their needs and receive relevant information, creating a more personalized and interactive experience. 3. **Time and Cost Savings**: By automating certain customer support processes, ChatGPT reduces the need for human intervention. This can result in significant time and cost savings for SAAS companies, allowing them to allocate resources more efficiently. 4. **Scalability**: ChatGPT's ability to handle multiple conversations simultaneously makes it highly scalable. It can cater to a large user base without compromising the quality of responses, ensuring a seamless experience even during peak usage periods. 5. **Data Collection and Analysis**: Through interactions with users, ChatGPT collects valuable data that can be used to gain insights into user preferences, pain points, and trends. This data can inform product improvements and marketing strategies, enabling SAAS companies to make data-driven decisions. ## Integrating ChatGPT into SAAS Applications Integrating ChatGPT into SAAS applications is made possible through OpenAI's API. The API allows developers to send user messages to ChatGPT and receive model-generated responses. Here are some key considerations for successful integration: 1. **Context Management**: Providing context to ChatGPT is crucial for generating meaningful responses. By maintaining context, the model can better understand the user's needs and provide accurate and relevant information. 2. **Error Handling**: While ChatGPT is a powerful language model, it can sometimes produce incorrect or nonsensical responses. Implementing error handling mechanisms, such as flagging potential errors or fallback options, ensures a smoother user experience. 3. **User Feedback**: Encouraging users to provide feedback on ChatGPT's responses can help improve the model's performance over time. SAAS companies can gather user feedback to identify areas for improvement and refine the model's responses accordingly. By effectively integrating ChatGPT into SAAS applications, businesses can unlock its potential to enhance customer support, improve user engagement, and streamline operations. The following chapters will delve into the technical aspects of integrating ChatGPT and provide actionable steps for developers and SAAS entrepreneurs. Remember, ChatGPT is a powerful tool, but it is essential to carefully consider its limitations and user experience implications when integrating it into SAAS applications. Stay tuned for the next chapter, where we will explore the practical aspects of integrating ChatGPT into SAAS applications.

# Chapter 6: How ChatGPT Works with SAAS

As we delve deeper into the world of no code SAAS applications, it's essential to explore how artificial intelligence (AI) technologies can enhance these applications. One such AI technology is ChatGPT, a powerful language model developed by OpenAI. In this chapter, we will discuss how ChatGPT works with SAAS and the numerous benefits it brings to the table.

## UNDERSTANDING CHATGPT

Before we dive into its integration with SAAS, let's gain a solid understanding of what ChatGPT is and its capabilities. ChatGPT is a cutting-edge language model that uses deep learning techniques to understand and generate natural language responses. It has been trained on a vast amount of data to enable it to engage in human-like conversations. One of the remarkable features of ChatGPT is its ability to generate coherent and contextually relevant responses, making it an ideal tool for chat-based interactions. From answering questions and providing suggestions to simulating dialogue, ChatGPT can perform a wide range of language-related tasks.

# BENEFITS OF INTEGRATING CHATGPT WITH SAAS

Now that we have a basic understanding of ChatGPT, let's explore the benefits it brings when integrated with SAAS applications:

## 1. Enhanced Customer Support

ChatGPT can revolutionize customer support for SAAS applications by providing instant and accurate responses to user queries. Its natural language processing capabilities allow it to understand user inputs and generate helpful responses. By integrating ChatGPT into a SAAS application's chat support system, businesses can provide round-the-clock assistance and improve customer satisfaction.

## 2. Improved User Engagement

By incorporating ChatGPT into a SAAS application, developers can create interactive and engaging user experiences. ChatGPT can simulate conversations and provide personalized recommendations, making the application more enticing for users. This increased engagement can lead to higher user retention rates and improved overall user satisfaction.

# 3. Time and Cost Savings

Integrating ChatGPT into a SAAS application can help automate certain tasks that would otherwise require human intervention. For example, ChatGPT can handle common support queries, reducing the workload on customer support teams. This automation saves both time and resources, allowing businesses to allocate their resources more efficiently.

# 4. Scalability

As SAAS applications grow in popularity and gain a larger user base, the demand for customer support also increases. ChatGPT's scalability allows it to handle multiple conversations simultaneously, ensuring a seamless experience for users. Businesses can scale their customer support operations without worrying about overwhelming their support teams.

# 5. Data Collection and Analysis

When users interact with ChatGPT, valuable data is generated. This data can be analyzed to gain insights into user behavior, preferences, and pain points. By integrating ChatGPT into a SAAS application, businesses can collect and leverage this data to make informed decisions about product enhancements, marketing strategies, and customer support improvements.

# INTEGRATING CHATGPT WITH SAAS

Integrating ChatGPT with a SAAS application is made possible through OpenAI's API, which provides developers with the necessary tools and interfaces to connect with ChatGPT. By leveraging the API, developers can create seamless integration points within their SAAS applications, enabling users to interact with ChatGPT effortlessly. However, successful integration requires careful consideration of several key factors, including context management, error handling, and user feedback. Context management ensures that ChatGPT understands and responds appropriately to ongoing conversations. Error handling ensures that ChatGPT gracefully handles situations where it might not understand the user's query or generates incorrect responses. User feedback is crucial for continuously improving ChatGPT's accuracy and performance.

# CONCLUSION

Integrating ChatGPT with SAAS applications opens up a world of possibilities, from enhancing customer support to improving user engagement and saving time and resources. By harnessing the power of AI and natural language processing, businesses can elevate their SAAS applications to new heights. In the next chapter, we will delve into the specifics of building your first no code SAAS application.

# Chapter 7: Integrating ChatGPT in SAAS Applications

Integrating ChatGPT, an AI-powered language model developed by OpenAI, into SAAS (Software as a Service) applications can provide numerous benefits, including enhanced customer support, improved user engagement, time and cost savings, scalability, and data collection and analysis. In this chapter, we will explore the process of integrating ChatGPT into SAAS applications and discuss key considerations for successful implementation.

## UNDERSTANDING CHATGPT

Before diving into the integration process, it is essential to understand the capabilities of ChatGPT. ChatGPT is designed to understand and generate natural language responses, providing users with an interactive conversational experience. It leverages OpenAI's advanced language generation models trained on vast amounts of data and can generate coherent and contextually relevant responses.

# BENEFITS OF INTEGRATING CHATGPT WITH SAAS

Integrating ChatGPT into SAAS applications offers several advantages for both businesses and users:

## Enhanced Customer Support

With ChatGPT, businesses can provide 24/7 customer support, ensuring that users receive assistance whenever they need it. ChatGPT can understand user queries and provide accurate and relevant responses, improving the overall customer experience.

## Improved User Engagement

By integrating ChatGPT, SAAS applications can offer interactive and engaging experiences to users. Chatbots powered by ChatGPT can hold conversations, answer questions, and provide recommendations, making the user experience more enjoyable and personalized.

## Time and Cost Savings

Integrating ChatGPT can automate repetitive tasks, such as answering frequently asked questions or providing basic guidance. This automation saves time and reduces the need for manual intervention, resulting in cost savings for businesses.

# Scalability

ChatGPT can handle a high volume of conversations simultaneously, allowing SAAS applications to scale their customer support without increasing staffing requirements. This scalability ensures that businesses can efficiently handle user inquiries, even during peak times.

# Data Collection and Analysis

Integrating ChatGPT enables the collection of valuable user data, which can be analyzed to gain insights into customer preferences, pain points, and behavior patterns. This data-driven approach empowers businesses to make informed decisions and enhance their SAAS offerings.

# INTEGRATING CHATGPT WITH SAAS APPLICATIONS

To integrate ChatGPT into SAAS applications, developers can utilize OpenAI's API, which provides a seamless way to interact with the language model. By following these general steps, businesses can successfully integrate ChatGPT into their SAAS applications:

# Step 1: Setting Up the API

Start by signing up for OpenAI's API and obtaining the necessary keys and credentials. This process typically involves creating an account, agreeing to the terms of service, and acquiring an API key.

# Step 2: Defining Use Cases

Identify the specific use cases for ChatGPT within the SAAS application. Determine where chat interactions would add value, such as customer support, onboarding assistance, or recommendation systems.

# Step 3: Designing Chat Interfaces

Create user-friendly chat interfaces that allow users to interact with ChatGPT seamlessly. Consider designing interfaces that provide context, enable error handling, and gather user feedback.

# Step 4: Implementing ChatGPT API Calls

Utilize the ChatGPT API to make requests and receive responses. This integration typically involves sending a user's message to the API and receiving a response that can be displayed to the user.

# Step 5: Context Management and Error Handling

Ensure proper context management when interacting with ChatGPT. Maintain the flow of conversation by passing previous messages or relevant information to provide context for accurate responses. Implement error handling mechanisms for cases where ChatGPT might generate incorrect or nonsensical answers.

## Step 6: User Feedback and Iterative Improvement

Collect user feedback to continuously improve the performance of ChatGPT. Evaluate user satisfaction, identify areas for enhancement, and refine the system accordingly.

## CONCLUSION

Integrating ChatGPT into SAAS applications can revolutionize customer support, enhance user engagement, and streamline operations. By leveraging the power of AI-powered conversational interfaces, businesses can unlock new possibilities and deliver exceptional user experiences. In the next chapter, we will delve further into the process of building a no-code SAAS application.

# Chapter 8: Building Your First No Code SAAS Application

Building a software-as-a-service (SAAS) application without any coding may sound like a daunting task, but with the rise of no code platforms, it has become more accessible and achievable for non-technical individuals and business owners. In this chapter, we will explore the step-by-step process of building your first no code SAAS application and turning your idea into a reality.

# 1. DEFINE YOUR APPLICATION'S PURPOSE AND TARGET AUDIENCE

Before diving into the development process, it's crucial to have a clear understanding of your application's purpose and the target audience you intend to serve. Consider the problem your application will solve and identify the specific pain points of your target users. This will serve as a guiding force throughout the development process.

# 2. RESEARCH NO CODE PLATFORMS

The next step is to research and evaluate different no code platforms that align with your project requirements. There are various no code platforms available in the market, each offering unique features and functionalities. Some popular no code platforms include Bubble, Adalo, OutSystems, and Webflow. Evaluate these platforms based on factors such as ease of use, scalability, available integrations, and pricing.

# 3. SELECT THE RIGHT TOOLS AND COMPONENTS

Once you have chosen a no code platform, explore the available tools and components that can help you bring your vision to life. No code platforms often provide a wide range of pre-built templates, layouts, and modules that can be customized to match your application's requirements. Take advantage of these resources to save time and effort during the development process.

# 4. DESIGN YOUR APPLICATION'S USER INTERFACE

User interface design plays a vital role in the success of any SAAS application. It directly impacts user experience and engagement. With no code platforms, designing an attractive and intuitive user interface becomes easier. Leverage the drag-and-drop functionality and visual editors offered by these platforms to create an interface that is visually appealing and user-friendly.

# 5. CUSTOMIZE AND CONFIGURE FUNCTIONALITY

No code platforms provide a range of built-in functionalities that can be easily customized and configured according to your application's needs. Identify the core features and functionality required for your SAAS application, such as user registration, data storage, payment processing, and analytics. Utilize the platform's available components and configuration options to tailor these functionalities to your specific requirements.

## 6. TEST AND ITERATE

Thorough testing is crucial to ensure the stability and functionality of your SAAS application. Use the testing capabilities provided by the no code platform to identify and fix any bugs or issues. Additionally, gather feedback from early users and iterate on your application to improve its performance and user experience.

# 7. DEPLOY AND LAUNCH YOUR SAAS APPLICATION

Once you are satisfied with the functionality and user experience of your SAAS application, it's time to deploy and launch it to the public. No code platforms often offer seamless deployment options, allowing you to publish your application with just a few clicks. Ensure that your chosen platform provides the necessary scalability and security features to handle increasing user demand and protect user data.

# 8. CONTINUE TO IMPROVE AND SCALE

Building your first no code SAAS application is just the beginning of your journey. The key to success in the SAAS industry is to continuously improve and scale your application based on user feedback and market demands. Regularly update your application, add new features, and optimize its performance to keep your users engaged and satisfied.

# CONCLUSION

Building your first no code SAAS application is an exciting and empowering journey. With the right platform, tools, and mindset, you can bring your ideas to life without the need for complex coding. Embrace the possibilities of no code development and take advantage of the opportunities it presents to create innovative and profitable SAAS applications.

# Chapter 9: Monetizing Your SAAS Application

Monetizing your software-as-a-service (SAAS) application is a crucial step in ensuring the financial success of your venture. While creating a valuable SAAS product is essential, it is equally important to establish sustainable revenue streams that will support your ongoing development, maintenance, and growth. In this chapter, we will explore various strategies for monetizing your SAAS application effectively.

## 1. SUBSCRIPTION MODEL

The subscription model is one of the most popular monetization strategies for SAAS applications. It involves offering different subscription plans with varying features and pricing tiers. Customers pay a recurring fee, typically on a monthly or annual basis, to access the software and its updates. When implementing a subscription model, it is crucial to define your pricing structure carefully. Consider factors such as the value your SAAS application provides, the target market's willingness to pay, and the competitive landscape. It might be beneficial to offer multiple pricing tiers to cater to different customer segments and maximize revenue potential.

# 2. USAGE-BASED PRICING

Another monetization approach is the usage-based pricing model, where customers are charged based on the extent of their usage. This model works well for SAAS applications that have varying levels of usage or consumption, such as communication tools or data processing platforms. By aligning the pricing with the customers' usage, you can provide a flexible and scalable payment structure. However, it is essential to strike a balance between fair pricing and ensuring profitability for your SAAS business.

# 3. FREEMIUM

The freemium model offers a basic version of your SAAS application for free, with limited features or usage rights. Customers can then upgrade to a paid version to access additional functionalities or remove restrictions. This model helps attract a large user base and allows customers to experience the value of your SAAS application before committing to a purchase. To make the freemium model successful, it is essential to provide enough value in the free version to engage users and convert them into paying customers. Additionally, focus on providing an exceptional user experience to differentiate your paid offerings and incentivize upgrades.

# 4. ONE-TIME PURCHASE

While less common for SAAS applications, the one-time purchase model involves selling the software for a fixed, upfront price. Customers pay for perpetual access to the software and may receive updates or support for a limited period. This approach can be suitable for niche or specialized SAAS applications that cater to a specific audience willing to make a significant upfront investment. However, keep in mind that ongoing support and updates may require additional revenue streams to sustain the long-term profitability of your SAAS business.

# 5. ADD-ONS AND UPSELLS

To increase your revenue potential, consider offering add-ons or upsells within your SAAS application. These are additional features or services that customers can purchase to enhance their experience or access advanced functionalities. By providing valuable add-ons, you can increase customer satisfaction and retention while generating incremental revenue. Look for opportunities to bundle complementary features or offer premium tiers for customers who require more advanced capabilities.

# 6. PARTNER PROGRAMS

Creating partner programs or reseller agreements can help extend the reach of your SAAS application and generate additional revenue. By partnering with other businesses, you can leverage their existing customer base and distribution channels to promote and sell your software. Under this model, you can offer revenue-sharing or commission-based arrangements with your partners, ensuring a mutually beneficial relationship. Collaborating with trusted partners can help increase your SAAS application's visibility and attract new customers.

## Conclusion

Monetizing your SAAS application requires careful consideration of your target market, pricing strategy, and the value you deliver to customers. A combination of different monetization models, such as subscriptions, usage-based pricing, freemium, one-time purchases, add-ons, and partner programs, can help you maximize revenue while catering to a diverse range of customers. Continuously monitor and evaluate your monetization strategy to adapt to market changes and optimize the financial sustainability of your SAAS business.

# Chapter 10: Pricing Models for SAAS Applications

When building a software-as-a-service (SAAS) application, one of the critical decisions that entrepreneurs need to make is determining the pricing model. The pricing model determines how customers will pay for and access your SAAS application, playing a vital role in revenue generation and customer acquisition. In this chapter, we will explore various pricing models commonly used by

SAAS businesses and discuss their advantages and considerations.

# 1. SUBSCRIPTION MODEL

The subscription model is the most popular pricing model for SAAS applications. In this model, customers pay a recurring fee (usually monthly or annually) to access and use the software. Subscription models generally offer different tiers or plans with varying features, functionality, and support levels. One advantage of the subscription model is the predictable and recurring revenue stream it provides. This allows SAAS companies to forecast their revenue and plan for growth more effectively. Additionally, a subscription model provides a steady cash flow and encourages customer retention, as customers are incentivized to continue their subscription to maintain access to the software. Considerations when using a subscription model include pricing the different tiers carefully to align with the value provided. It is important to strike a balance between providing enough features to justify a higher-priced tier while giving a compelling entry-level option to attract new customers. Additionally, monitoring and understanding customer usage patterns can help refine pricing and ensure customers feel they are getting value for their subscription.

# 2. USAGE-BASED PRICING

Usage-based pricing is a model where customers are charged based on their actual usage or consumption of the

SAAS application. This model is particularly suitable for applications that involve data storage, data processing, or resource-intensive tasks. By charging customers based on usage, SAAS companies can align pricing with the value customers receive. The advantage of usage-based pricing is that customers only pay for what they use, making it a fair and transparent pricing model. This model also allows customers to start with a low-cost entry point and scale their usage as needed, providing flexibility and cost control. However, implementing usage-based pricing can be complex and requires accurate tracking and billing mechanisms. SAAS companies need to invest in robust metering and usage monitoring systems to accurately measure and bill customers for their usage. Additionally, clear communication and transparency around pricing and usage metrics are crucial to avoid customer dissatisfaction or confusion.

# 3. FREEMIUM MODEL

The freemium model is a pricing model where SAAS applications offer a free version with limited features and functionality, while charging for premium features or upgrades. The free version acts as a marketing tool to attract users and allows them to experience the core value of the application. SAAS companies can then upsell premium features or additional services to convert free users into paying customers. The freemium model can be an effective strategy for customer acquisition and user growth. By offering a free version, SAAS companies can lower the barrier to entry, encourage trial usage, and increase brand visibility. It also allows SAAS companies to showcase the value of their product and build a user base that can potentially convert to paying customers. To maximize the success of the freemium model, SAAS companies need to carefully identify the features that are valuable enough to be included in the premium version. It is important to strike a balance between providing enough value in the free version to attract users and offering compelling premium features that drive conversion.

# 4. ONE-TIME PURCHASE MODEL

While less common in SAAS applications, the one-time purchase model involves customers paying a single upfront fee to purchase and use the software indefinitely. This model is often used for niche SAAS applications or products with limited ongoing support or maintenance requirements. The advantage of the one-time purchase model is that it can provide immediate revenue and cash flow. SAAS companies receive payment upfront, which can be beneficial for startups or businesses that require capital to fund further development or expansion. Additionally, customers have full ownership of the software and can use it without ongoing subscription fees. However, the one-time purchase model may not be suitable for all SAAS applications. Ongoing customer support, maintenance, and software updates may incur costs that need to be factored in. SAAS companies need to carefully consider the balance between one-time revenue and ongoing support efforts to ensure long-term success.

# 5. ADD-ONS AND UPSELLS

Another pricing model approach is to offer add-ons and upsells to enhance the customer experience and provide additional value. SAAS companies can offer optional features, modules, or services as add-ons to the base software or as standalone offerings. Add-ons and upsells can be an effective way to generate additional revenue and cater to customers with specific needs. SAAS companies can analyze customer usage patterns and preferences to identify potential upselling opportunities. By offering relevant add-ons, SAAS companies can provide a more tailored solution and increase customer satisfaction. It is crucial to ensure pricing for add-ons and upsells is carefully aligned with the value they provide. Customers should feel that the additional features or services are worth the extra cost and enhance their overall experience with the SAAS application.

# 6. PARTNER PROGRAMS/RESELLER AGREEMENTS

Partner programs or reseller agreements provide opportunities for SAAS companies to expand their reach and revenue generation through partnerships with other businesses. SAAS companies can collaborate with value-added resellers, consultants, or other strategic partners to sell and distribute their software to a broader customer base. Partner programs can have various pricing models, such as revenue-sharing agreements, upfront fees, or commission-based structures. The specific pricing model will depend on the nature of the partnership and the roles and responsibilities of each party. Partner programs and reseller agreements can be beneficial for SAAS companies looking to scale their business without significant upfront investment in sales and marketing efforts. These partnerships allow SAAS companies to tap into existing networks and leverage the expertise and customer relationships of their partners. In conclusion, selecting the right pricing model for your SAAS application is a critical decision that influences revenue generation, customer acquisition, and overall business success. Each pricing model has its advantages and considerations, and it is essential to align the pricing strategy with the value provided to customers. SAAS companies should analyze their target market, understand customer preferences, and continuously evaluate and refine pricing models to ensure profitability and customer satisfaction.

# Chapter 11: Marketing Your No Code SAAS Application

Marketing plays a crucial role in the success of any software-as-a-service (SAAS) application, including those built using no code platforms. Effective marketing strategies help generate awareness, attract potential customers, and drive user adoption. In this chapter, we will explore various marketing strategies and tactics that can help you promote your no code SAAS application and achieve long-term growth.

# 1. DEFINE YOUR TARGET AUDIENCE

Before you start marketing your SAAS application, it is important to clearly define your target audience. Understanding who your ideal customers are will enable you to tailor your marketing messages and reach the right people. Consider factors such as industry, company size, job role, and pain points that your application addresses. This information will guide your marketing efforts and help you create targeted campaigns.

# 2. DEVELOP A COMPELLING VALUE PROPOSITION

A strong value proposition is essential for attracting and convincing potential customers to choose your no code SAAS application. Clearly communicate the unique features and benefits of your application, highlighting how it solves a specific problem or addresses a pain point. Focus on the value it brings to your customers and how it can improve their workflow, efficiency, or productivity. A compelling value proposition will set you apart from competitors and resonate with your target audience.

# 3. CREATE AN ENGAGING WEBSITE

Your website serves as the digital storefront for your SAAS application. It is important to create an engaging, user-friendly website that effectively communicates your value proposition and showcases the features and benefits of your application. Use high-quality visuals, compelling copywriting, and clear call-to-action buttons to guide visitors towards signing up or learning more about your product. Optimize your website for search engines to improve its visibility and attract organic traffic.

# 4. CONTENT MARKETING

Content marketing is a powerful strategy for building brand awareness, establishing thought leadership, and attracting potential customers. Create valuable content such as blog posts, whitepapers, case studies, and videos that address common pain points or provide useful insights related to your industry. Share this content on your website, social media platforms, and relevant industry forums. By providing valuable information, you can position yourself as an authority in the field and build trust with your target audience.

# 5. SOCIAL MEDIA MARKETING

Social media platforms provide a valuable opportunity to engage with your target audience and build a community around your SAAS application. Identify the social media platforms that your target audience frequents and create a strong presence there. Share updates, industry news, customer testimonials, and valuable content to engage with your audience. Utilize paid advertising options on social media platforms to reach a wider audience and drive traffic to your website.

# 6. INFLUENCER MARKETING

Influencer marketing can be an effective strategy for reaching a larger audience and gaining credibility for your SAAS application. Identify influencers or thought leaders in your industry who have a significant following and align with your target audience. Collaborate with them to create content, run joint webinars or events, or have them review and endorse your application. This can help increase brand visibility, attract new customers, and build trust among your target audience.

# 7. REFERRAL PROGRAMS

Referral programs can be a powerful marketing tool to encourage your existing customers to refer your SAAS application to their network. Offer incentives such as discounts, extended trial periods, or exclusive features to customers who refer new users. Implement a referral tracking system to keep track of referrals and reward customers accordingly. By leveraging the networks and trust of your existing customers, you can rapidly expand your user base.

# 8. USER REVIEWS AND TESTIMONIALS

Positive user reviews and testimonials can significantly influence potential customers' decision-making process. Encourage your satisfied customers to leave reviews on popular review websites or provide testimonials for your website. Consider offering incentives or discounts to customers who provide reviews. Display these testimonials prominently on your website and in your marketing materials to build trust and credibility.

# 9. EMAIL MARKETING

Email marketing is a powerful tool for nurturing leads, improving customer retention, and driving conversions. Build an email list of interested prospects and existing customers. Send regular newsletters, product updates, industry insights, and promotional offers to keep your audience engaged and informed. Use personalized email marketing to provide relevant content and offers based on user behavior and preferences. Monitor email engagement metrics to optimize your campaigns and improve conversion rates.

## 10. ANALYZE AND REFINE YOUR MARKETING EFFORTS

Regularly analyze the performance of your marketing efforts and refine your strategies based on the data. Track key metrics such as website traffic, conversion rates, customer acquisition cost, and customer churn rate. Use tools like Google Analytics and marketing automation platforms to gain insights into user behavior and engagement. Experiment with different marketing channels, messaging, and targeting techniques to identify what works best for your SAAS application. In conclusion, marketing your no code SAAS application requires a comprehensive and strategic approach. By defining your target audience, developing a compelling value proposition, creating engaging marketing materials, and leveraging various channels such as content marketing, social media, influencer marketing, and email marketing, you can effectively promote your application and drive user adoption. Constantly analyze and refine your marketing efforts to optimize your strategies and fuel long-term growth for your SAAS business.

# Chapter 12: Growing Your User Base

Growing your user base is a crucial step in achieving success with your no code SAAS application. The more users you have, the more revenue you can generate and the stronger your position in the market becomes. In this chapter, we will explore strategies and tactics to help you effectively grow your user base.

# 1. USER ACQUISITION STRATEGIES

User acquisition refers to the process of acquiring new users for your SAAS application. Here are some effective strategies to consider:

## a. Content Marketing

Content marketing involves creating and sharing valuable content that attracts and engages your target audience. This can include blog posts, videos, tutorials, case studies, and more. By providing valuable information and insights, you can position yourself as an authority in the industry and attract users to your SAAS application.

## b. Social Media Marketing

Social media platforms provide excellent opportunities to reach and engage with your target audience. Develop a strong presence on platforms such as Facebook, Twitter, LinkedIn, and Instagram. Regularly share content, engage with your audience, and use targeted advertising to drive traffic to your SAAS application.

## c. Influencer Marketing

Collaborating with influencers who have a significant following in your target market can help you reach a wider audience and gain credibility. Identify relevant influencers and establish partnerships to promote your SAAS application to their followers.

## d. Referral Programs

Implementing referral programs can incentivize your existing users to refer your SAAS application to their networks. Offer rewards or discounts for successful referrals to encourage users to spread the word about your application.

## e. Search Engine Optimization (SEO)

Optimizing your website and content for search engines can help drive organic traffic to your SAAS application. Research relevant keywords, optimize your website's meta tags, create high-quality content, and build backlinks to improve your search engine rankings.

## 2. USER ENGAGEMENT AND RETENTION

While acquiring new users is essential, it's equally important to focus on user engagement and retention.

Here's how you can keep your existing users engaged and increase their loyalty:

# a. Personalization and Customization

Offer personalized experiences and customization options to make your users feel valued. Allow them to tailor the application to their preferences and provide relevant recommendations based on their usage patterns.

# b. Regular Updates and Enhancements

Continuously improve your SAAS application by releasing regular updates and adding new features. Show your users that you are actively working to enhance their experience and address their needs.

# c. Proactive Customer Support

Provide exceptional customer support by being responsive, proactive, and helpful. Address user queries and concerns promptly, offer self-service resources, and consider implementing a chatbot or AI-powered assistant to provide instant assistance.

# d. Gamification

Incorporate gamification elements into your SAAS application to make it more engaging and enjoyable for your users. Implement features such as badges, leaderboards, and rewards to encourage user interaction and loyalty.

# 3. USER FEEDBACK AND ITERATIVE IMPROVEMENT

Regularly gather user feedback to identify areas for improvement and address any pain points or challenges users may be facing. Conduct surveys, analyze user behavior data, and encourage users to provide feedback and suggest enhancements. Use this feedback to iterate and continually improve your SAAS application.

# 4. PARTNERSHIP AND COLLABORATIONS

Collaborating with other businesses, influencers, or industry experts can help you reach a broader audience and gain credibility. Look for partnership opportunities such as co-marketing campaigns, guest blogging, webinars, or joint ventures to tap into new user bases and expand your reach.

# CONCLUSION

Growing your user base is a continuous process that requires strategic planning, implementation of effective marketing strategies, and a strong focus on user engagement and retention. By applying the strategies mentioned in this chapter, you can successfully expand your user base and drive the growth of your no code SAAS application.

# Chapter 13: Retaining Customers for Long-Term Success

## THE IMPORTANCE OF CUSTOMER RETENTION

Retaining customers is essential for the long-term success of your SAAS application. Not only does it ensure a steady stream of revenue, but it also helps you build a loyal customer base and a positive brand reputation. Customer retention is more cost-effective than acquiring new customers, as it involves less marketing and sales expenses. Additionally, loyal customers are more likely to recommend your SAAS application to others, helping you expand your user base.

# STRATEGIES FOR CUSTOMER RETENTION

To effectively retain customers, you need to focus on providing value, building strong relationships, and continuously improving your SAAS application. Here are some strategies to help you retain customers for the long term:

## 1. Offer Exceptional Customer Support

Providing excellent customer support is crucial for customer retention. Your support team should be responsive, knowledgeable, and accessible via multiple channels such as live chat, email, and phone. Respond to customer inquiries promptly and aim to resolve issues quickly and efficiently. Implementing self-service options, such as a comprehensive knowledge base or a community forum, can also empower customers to find solutions on their own.

## 2. Provide Regular Updates and Enhancements

Regularly releasing updates and enhancements to your SAAS application demonstrates your commitment to improving the user experience. Keep track of customer feedback and prioritize feature requests and bug fixes accordingly. Communicate these updates with your customers through release notes or newsletters to show that you are actively working to meet their needs.

# 3. Personalization and Customization

Allowing customers to customize and personalize their experience within your SAAS application can enhance their satisfaction and loyalty. Provide options for them to tailor settings, preferences, and workflows to their specific needs. This customization empowers customers to create a personalized experience that aligns with their unique requirements.

# 4. Proactive Customer Outreach

Don't wait for customers to reach out to you with issues or concerns. Proactively engage with your customers to ensure their satisfaction and address any potential problems before they escalate. Regularly send out surveys or feedback forms to gather insights on customer experiences. Actively solicit feedback and use it to improve your SAAS application and customer service.

# 5. Loyalty Programs and Rewards

Implementing a loyalty program can incentivize customers to stay with your SAAS application in the long run. Offer exclusive benefits, discounts, or rewards to customers who have been with you for a certain period or have reached a specific usage milestone. These rewards can range from access to premium features, discounted pricing, or even personalized support.

# MONITORING CUSTOMER RETENTION METRICS

To measure the effectiveness of your customer retention strategies, it's important to monitor key metrics. Some essential metrics to track include: - Churn Rate: The rate at which customers cancel their subscriptions or stop using your SAAS application. - Customer Lifetime Value (CLTV): The total revenue generated by a customer throughout their entire relationship with your SAAS application. - Net Promoter Score (NPS): A measure of customer loyalty and likelihood to recommend your SAAS application to others. - Customer Satisfaction (CSAT) Score: The satisfaction level of your customers based on surveys or feedback. Continuously monitor and analyze these metrics to identify trends, areas for improvement, and the overall health of your customer base.

# IN SUMMARY

Retaining customers is vital for the long-term success of your SAAS application. By focusing on exceptional customer support, regular updates, personalization, proactive customer outreach, and loyalty programs, you can foster strong relationships and loyalty among your customers. Additionally, monitoring customer retention metrics will help you gauge the effectiveness of your strategies and make data-driven decisions to improve customer retention efforts.

# Chapter 14: Scaling Your SAAS Business

Scaling your SAAS (Software-as-a-Service) business is crucial for long-term success and to meet the growing demands of your customers. As your user base expands and your software gains more traction in the market, it becomes essential to scale your infrastructure, processes, and team to ensure seamless operations and continued growth. In this chapter, we will explore strategies and best practices for effectively scaling your SAAS business.

## THE IMPORTANCE OF SCALING

Scaling your SAAS business refers to the process of increasing the capacity and capabilities of your operations to accommodate the growing user base, handle increased workload, and meet customer expectations. Scaling is crucial for several reasons: **1. Meeting Customer Demand:** As your SAAS application gains popularity, the demand from users will increase. Scaling ensures that you can handle the influx of new users and provide a seamless experience to all customers. **2. Improving Performance:** Scaling enables you to optimize your infrastructure and resources, ensuring maximum performance and minimal downtime. This is especially important for SAAS applications that require high availability and responsiveness. **3. Accommodating Growth:** Scaling allows your business to grow and expand without being limited by technical or operational constraints. It enables you to capture new market opportunities and increase your revenue potential. **4. Staying Competitive:** In the fast-paced SAAS industry, it is crucial to keep up with competitors and meet evolving customer expectations. Scaling allows you to innovate, introduce new features, and stay ahead of the competition.

# STRATEGIES FOR SCALING YOUR SAAS BUSINESS

Scaling a SAAS business involves multiple aspects, including infrastructure, processes, team, and customer success. Here are strategies to consider when scaling your SAAS business: **1. Infrastructure Scaling:** Evaluate your current infrastructure and make sure it can handle increased traffic and usage. Consider using cloud services like Amazon Web Services (AWS), Microsoft Azure, or Google Cloud Platform to scale your infrastructure on-demand. Use load balancers, auto-scaling, and caching techniques to optimize performance. **2. Architecture Redesign:** Assess your application's architecture and make necessary changes to ensure scalability. Moving to a microservices or serverless architecture can help distribute the workload and improve fault tolerance. **3. Process Automation:** Implement automation tools and workflows to streamline manual processes and reduce human intervention. Automating tasks like deployment, testing, and data analysis can save time and resources. **4. Agile**

**Development:** Embrace agile principles and methodologies to iterate quickly and efficiently. Break down development tasks into small, manageable chunks and prioritize based on customer needs. Emphasize continuous integration and deployment to release new features and updates faster. **5. Outsourcing and Partnerships:** Consider outsourcing non-core activities or partnering with external service providers to leverage their expertise and resources. This can help you scale efficiently while focusing on your core product development. **6. Team Development:** As your business scales, you may need to expand your team. Hire talented individuals who align with your company culture and possess the necessary skills. Foster a collaborative and productive work environment to ensure smooth operations. **7. Customer Success and Support:** Invest in a robust customer success and support team to ensure high customer satisfaction. Provide self-service resources, proactive customer outreach, and quick response times to address any issues or concerns.

# MEASURING AND MONITORING SCALING SUCCESS

To ensure successful scaling, it is essential to measure and monitor key metrics. Here are some metrics to consider: 1. **Usage and Adoption:** Monitor the number of active users, user engagement, and feature adoption rates to gauge the success and impact of your scaling efforts. 2. **Response Time and Performance:** Measure your application's response time and performance under increasing loads.

Ensure that your infrastructure and optimizations can handle the growing demands. 3. **Churn Rate:** Track the rate at which customers are leaving your SAAS application. A high churn rate may indicate issues with scaling or customer satisfaction. 4. **Revenue Growth:** Monitor your revenue growth as a result of scaling. Measure the increase in paying customers, average revenue per user (ARPU), and overall revenue. 5. **Customer Satisfaction:** Regularly collect and analyze customer feedback to gauge satisfaction levels. Use metrics like Net Promoter Score (NPS) and Customer Satisfaction Score (CSAT) to assess the overall customer sentiment. By regularly assessing these metrics, you can identify bottlenecks, measure the effectiveness of your scaling efforts, and make data-driven decisions to further optimize your SAAS business.

# CONCLUSION

Scaling your SAAS business is crucial to accommodate the growing demands of your customers and to stay competitive in the market. By implementing effective scaling strategies, optimizing your infrastructure and processes, and prioritizing customer success, you can ensure seamless operations, improved performance, and continued growth. Regular monitoring of key metrics will provide insights into the success of your scaling efforts and guide future decision-making.

# Chapter 15: Lessons from Successful No Code SAAS Entrepreneurs

## INTRODUCTION

Successful entrepreneurs in the no code SAAS industry have paved the way for aspiring individuals and businesses to achieve their own success. Their innovations, strategies, and insights provide valuable lessons that can be applied to building and growing no code SAAS applications. In this chapter, we will explore some of the key lessons from these successful entrepreneurs and how you can implement them in your own journey towards becoming a no code SAAS millionaire.

## LESSON 1: START WITH A PROBLEM

One of the common themes among successful no code SAAS entrepreneurs is that they started by identifying a problem that needed solving. They observed pain points or inefficiencies in existing processes and sought to create a solution that would address these challenges. This lesson teaches us the importance of conducting thorough market research and understanding the needs and pain points of your target audience before diving into application development. By starting with a problem, you ensure that there is a market demand for your SAAS application. It also allows you to differentiate yourself from competitors and provide a unique value proposition to your customers.

# LESSON 2: BUILD SIMPLE AND INTUITIVE APPLICATIONS

Another valuable lesson from successful no code SAAS entrepreneurs is the importance of building simple and intuitive applications. They understand that user experience is key to the success of any SAAS application. By prioritizing ease of use and intuitive design, they create applications that can be adopted quickly and seamlessly by users. When building your no code SAAS application, focus on creating a user-friendly interface and streamlined workflows. Consider the needs and preferences of your target audience and remove any unnecessary complexity or barriers to entry. By making your application intuitive, you increase the likelihood of user adoption and satisfaction.

# LESSON 3: EMBRACE CONTINUOUS IMPROVEMENT

Successful entrepreneurs in the no code SAAS space recognize the importance of embracing continuous improvement. They understand that the market is constantly evolving, and customer demands and expectations are ever-changing. Rather than settling for mediocrity, they actively seek feedback from their users and iterate on their applications based on these insights. To apply this lesson, prioritize collecting user feedback and analyzing user data. Monitor key performance indicators (KPIs) such as user engagement, churn rate, and customer satisfaction. Use this data to identify areas for improvement and implement regular updates and enhancements to your application. By continuously improving your no code SAAS application, you not only meet the evolving needs of your customers but also stay ahead of the competition.

# LESSON 4: FOCUS ON CUSTOMER SUCCESS

Customer success is a core focus for successful no code SAAS entrepreneurs. They recognize that their customers' success directly correlates to their own success. By prioritizing customer satisfaction and providing exceptional support, these entrepreneurs build strong and lasting relationships with their user base. To implement this lesson, invest in providing excellent customer support and ensure that your customers have access to the resources they need to succeed. Proactively engage with your users, address their concerns, and provide timely assistance. By prioritizing customer success, you not only retain your existing customers but also attract new users through positive word-of-mouth referrals.

# LESSON 5: DEVELOP A STRONG BRAND AND MARKETING STRATEGY

Successful no code SAAS entrepreneurs understand the importance of developing a strong brand and marketing strategy. They invest in building a compelling brand story, creating a visually appealing and memorable brand identity, and implementing effective marketing tactics to reach their target audience. To apply this lesson, define your brand's unique value proposition and develop a consistent brand voice and identity. Create engaging content that resonates with your target audience through various marketing channels, such as social media, content marketing, and email marketing. Leverage the power of storytelling to connect with your audience on a deeper level and establish brand loyalty.

# CONCLUSION

By studying the lessons from successful no code SAAS entrepreneurs, you can gain valuable insights and guidance for your own journey. Start by identifying a problem, build simple and intuitive applications, embrace continuous improvement, prioritize customer success, and develop a strong brand and marketing strategy. By applying these lessons, you can increase the chances of achieving success as a no code SAAS entrepreneur and potentially become a millionaire in the industry.

# Chapter 17: Leveraging Automation in No Code SAAS

Automation plays a vital role in maximizing the efficiency and productivity of any business, and the world of no code SAAS is no exception. With the advancements in technology, automation has become increasingly accessible and powerful, offering numerous benefits to no code SAAS entrepreneurs. In this chapter, we will explore the importance of leveraging automation in the no code SAAS industry and how it can drive your business towards success.

## UNDERSTANDING AUTOMATION IN NO CODE SAAS

Automation refers to the process of using technology to perform tasks or processes without human intervention. In the context of no code SAAS, automation enables entrepreneurs to streamline and optimize their workflows, saving time and resources. It eliminates manual and repetitive tasks, allowing you to focus on more strategic and high-value activities.

# The Benefits of Automation

1. **Improved Efficiency:** Automation reduces the time and effort required to complete tasks, resulting in improved operational efficiency. By automating routine processes, you can eliminate human errors and ensure consistency in your operations. 2. **Cost Savings:** By automating repetitive tasks, you can reduce labor costs and allocate resources to more important aspects of your business. Automation minimizes the need for manual intervention, saving both time and money. 3. **Increase in Productivity:** With automation handling repetitive tasks, your team can focus on more value-added activities, such as product development, customer support, and business growth. This leads to increased productivity and the ability to accomplish more in less time. 4. **Enhanced Accuracy:** Human errors are inevitable, but automation can significantly reduce the chances of mistakes. By leveraging automation tools, you can ensure precision and accuracy in tasks such as data entry, report generation, and customer support. 5. **Scalability:** Automation allows you to scale your operations without the need for additional resources. As your business grows, automation can handle increased workloads, ensuring that your processes remain efficient and effective.

# IMPLEMENTING AUTOMATION IN NO CODE SAAS

To leverage automation effectively in your no code SAAS business, consider the following strategies: 1. **Identify areas for automation:** Evaluate your business processes and identify tasks that are repetitive, time-consuming, and prone to human error. These are the areas where automation can have the most significant impact. 2. **Choose the right automation tools:** Research and select automation tools that align with your business needs. There are various no code automation platforms available that allow you to automate workflows, integrate different applications, and create custom automations. 3. **Streamline workflows:** Once you have chosen your automation tools, map out your existing workflows and identify opportunities to automate. Look for tasks that can be automated, such as data entry, report generation, email marketing, and customer onboarding. 4. **Implement automation gradually:** Start by automating smaller tasks or processes to gain confidence in the automation tools and processes. As you become comfortable with automation, gradually expand its implementation to more complex workflows. 5. **Continuously monitor and improve:** Regularly review and analyze the performance of your automated processes. Gather feedback from your team and customers to identify areas for improvement. Automation is not a one-time solution; it requires ongoing refinement and optimization.

# THE FUTURE OF AUTOMATION IN NO CODE SAAS

As technology continues to advance, the potential for automation in the no code SAAS industry is vast. Artificial intelligence and machine learning capabilities are being integrated into automation tools, allowing for more intelligent and predictive automation. This can further enhance efficiency, accuracy, and decision-making in no code SAAS applications. Additionally, the integration of automation with other emerging technologies, such as robotic process automation (RPA) and Internet of Things (IoT), will unlock new possibilities for automating complex business processes and creating innovative solutions.

## Conclusion

Leveraging automation in the no code SAAS industry is essential for maximizing efficiency, productivity, and scalability. By automating repetitive tasks, you can streamline your workflows, reduce errors, and allocate resources more effectively. As technology continues to evolve, the potential for automation in no code SAAS applications will only grow, offering exciting opportunities for entrepreneurs to make their businesses more efficient and competitive. Embrace automation in your no code SAAS journey and unlock its transformative power for your business success.

# Chapter 17: Leveraging Automation in No Code SAAS

Automation plays a crucial role in the success of no code SAAS applications. By automating various tasks and processes, businesses can streamline workflows, improve efficiency, and scale their operations. In this chapter, we will explore the benefits of automation in the no code

SAAS industry and discuss strategies for effectively leveraging automation in your SAAS business.

# THE BENEFITS OF AUTOMATION

Automation offers numerous benefits for no code SAAS businesses. Here are some key advantages of leveraging automation:

## 1. Improved Efficiency

Automation eliminates the need for manual, repetitive tasks, allowing your team to focus on more strategic and value-added activities. By automating processes such as data entry, report generation, and system monitoring, you can save time and increase overall efficiency.

## 2. Cost Savings

Automating repetitive tasks can significantly reduce labor costs. Instead of hiring additional staff to handle manual tasks, automation enables you to allocate resources more effectively, saving money in the long run.

## 3. Increased Productivity

With automation, your team can accomplish more in less time. By eliminating the need to perform repetitive tasks manually, employees can allocate their time and energy to more creative and critical tasks, leading to increased productivity.

# 4. Enhanced Accuracy

Manual processes are prone to human errors, which can be costly and time-consuming to fix. By automating tasks, you can ensure consistent and accurate results, reducing the risk of errors and improving the quality of your outputs.

# 5. Scalability

As your SAAS business grows, automation allows you to scale your operations effortlessly. Automated processes can handle higher volumes of data and tasks without a significant increase in resources, enabling your business to accommodate growth seamlessly.

# STRATEGIES FOR IMPLEMENTING AUTOMATION

To effectively leverage automation in your no code SAAS business, consider the following strategies:

# 1. Identify Areas for Automation

Start by identifying the tasks and processes within your SAAS business that can benefit from automation. Look for repetitive, time-consuming tasks that can be systematized and streamlined through automation.

# 2. Choose the Right Automation Tools

There is a wide range of automation tools available for no code SAAS businesses. Research and select tools that align with your specific needs and requirements. Look for platforms that offer integrations with your existing systems and provide user-friendly interfaces for ease of use.

# 3. Streamline Workflows

Before implementing automation, streamline your workflows to ensure optimal efficiency. Removing unnecessary steps and simplifying processes will enable automation to have a more significant impact on your productivity.

# 4. Implement Automation Gradually

Instead of automating all processes at once, introduce automation gradually. This approach allows you to identify and address any potential issues or bottlenecks. Start with simpler tasks and gradually move on to more complex processes.

# 5. Continuously Monitor and Improve

Automation is not a one-time implementation. It requires regular monitoring and fine-tuning to ensure its effectiveness. Continuously monitor the performance of automated processes, collect feedback from users, and make improvements based on the insights gathered.

# THE FUTURE OF AUTOMATION IN NO CODE SAAS

The future of automation in no code SAAS is promising, with ongoing advancements in technology. Here are some trends to watch out for: - Integration with AI and Machine Learning: Automation can be enhanced by incorporating artificial intelligence and machine learning capabilities. This allows for more intelligent decision-making, predictive analytics, and the ability to learn from user behavior. - Robotic Process Automation (RPA): RPA involves the use of software robots or "bots" to automate repetitive, rule-based tasks. RPA can be leveraged in conjunction with no code platforms to further streamline workflows and improve efficiency. - Internet of Things (IoT): IoT devices can gather and transmit data, enabling automation in various industries. Integration of IoT devices with no code SAAS platforms can provide enhanced automation capabilities and real-time data-driven insights. - Enhanced Chatbot and Virtual Assistant Integration: Chatbots and virtual assistants powered by AI can automate customer support, help desk services, and other interactions. Integrating these technologies with no code SAAS platforms can provide enhanced customer experiences and support.

# LEVERAGING AUTOMATION FOR SUCCESS

In the rapidly evolving landscape of no code SAAS, leveraging automation is essential for maximizing efficiency, productivity, and scalability. By identifying areas for automation, choosing the right tools, streamlining workflows, and continuously improving processes, you can position your business for success in the no code SAAS industry. Embrace automation as a strategic tool and stay ahead of the competition by meeting customer demands effectively and efficiently.

# Chapter 18: Innovating and Staying Ahead in the No Code SAAS Industry

In the ever-evolving world of technology, it is crucial for SAAS entrepreneurs to constantly innovate and stay ahead of the competition. This is especially true in the no code SAAS industry, where advancements are being made at a rapid pace. In this chapter, we will explore strategies and best practices for innovating and staying ahead in the no code SAAS industry.

# INNOVATING IN THE NO CODE SAAS INDUSTRY

Innovation is the key to success in any industry, and the no code SAAS industry is no exception. Here are some strategies to help you stay at the forefront of innovation: 1. Stay updated with industry trends: Keep a close eye on the latest trends and developments in the no code SAAS industry. Attend conferences, read industry blogs, and join relevant online communities to stay informed about new tools, technologies, and best practices. 2. Foster a culture of innovation: Encourage your team to think outside the box and come up with innovative ideas. Create an environment that values creativity, experimentation, and continuous learning. Provide resources and support to turn those ideas into reality. 3. Collaborate with users and stakeholders: Engage with your users and stakeholders to understand their pain points, challenges, and needs. Conduct surveys, interviews, and user testing sessions to gather valuable insights. Use this feedback to inform your innovation strategy and prioritize feature development. 4. Stay agile and adaptable: Embrace an agile mindset that promotes flexibility and adaptability. Be open to change and willing to pivot when necessary. Stay nimble in your development process and iterate quickly based on user feedback and market demands. 5. Embrace emerging technologies: Keep an eye on emerging technologies that can complement and enhance your no code SAAS application. Explore the potential of artificial intelligence (AI), machine learning (ML), Internet of Things (IoT), and blockchain to add value and differentiate your offering.

# STAYING AHEAD IN THE NO CODE SAAS INDUSTRY

In addition to innovation, staying ahead of the competition requires strategic planning and a proactive mindset. Here are some tips to help you stay ahead in the no code SAAS industry: 1. Monitor the competitive landscape: Keep a close eye on your competitors to understand their offerings, pricing strategies, marketing tactics, and customer satisfaction levels. Identify gaps and opportunities where you can differentiate and outperform them. 2. Focus on customer experience: Delivering an exceptional customer experience is paramount in the no code SAAS industry. Continuously listen to your customers, gather feedback, and incorporate their suggestions to enhance your product offering. Provide exceptional customer support and build long-lasting relationships with your customers. 3. Embrace continuous improvement: Never settle for mediocrity. Continuously strive to improve your product, service, and internal processes. Regularly analyze and measure key performance indicators (KPIs) to identify areas for improvement. Implement agile methodologies to enable quick iterations and continuous delivery. 4. Invest in research and development: Allocate resources to research and development activities to explore new features, technologies, and improvements that can give you a competitive edge. Experiment with new ideas, test prototypes, and gather feedback from early adopters. 5. Build strategic partnerships: Collaborate with complementary businesses and form strategic partnerships that can expand your reach, enhance your product offering, and generate new revenue streams. Look for opportunities to integrate your no code SAAS application with other popular tools and platforms in the market. 6. Engage in thought leadership: Establish yourself as a thought leader in the no code SAAS industry by sharing your expertise through blog posts, webinars, podcasts, and speaking engagements. Contribute to relevant industry publications and participate in panel discussions to build your reputation and credibility. 7. Stay customer-centric: Always put your customers at the center of your decision-making process. Understand their needs, pain points, and challenges, and design your product and marketing strategies accordingly. Regularly seek feedback and engage in conversations with your customers to ensure you are delivering value. By consistently innovating and staying ahead in the no code SAAS industry, you can position yourself as a leader and create a sustainable competitive advantage. Remember to stay agile, listen to your customers, and leverage emerging technologies to drive innovation and success in your no code SAAS business. Next, we will explore the important considerations when building a team for your SAAS business.

# Chapter 19: Building a Team for Your SAAS Business

Building a strong and capable team is essential for the success of your SAAS business. As your business grows, you may find yourself needing to expand your team to meet the demands of your customers and market. In this chapter, we will explore the key considerations and strategies for building a team for your SAAS business.

# THE IMPORTANCE OF A STRONG TEAM

A strong team is the backbone of your SAAS business. They are responsible for the development, maintenance, and success of your software application. Here are some reasons why building a strong team is crucial: 1. Expertise and Skills: Hiring individuals with the right expertise and skills is vital to ensure smooth operations and high-quality outputs. Look for candidates with experience in software development, customer support, marketing, sales, and project management. 2. Collaboration and Communication: A cohesive and collaborative team fosters innovation, creativity, and efficient problem-solving. Encourage open communication and teamwork among team members to enhance productivity and synergy. 3. Scalability: As your business grows, you need a team that can scale alongside it. Hiring individuals who can adapt to changing responsibilities and workloads is essential to maintain momentum and meet customer demands. 4. Customer Satisfaction: A well-rounded team with strong customer-centric values will ensure that customer needs and expectations are met. A satisfied customer base leads to positive reviews, referrals, and long-term success.

# BUILDING YOUR SAAS TEAM

Here are some steps to consider when building your SAAS team:

## Identify Roles and Responsibilities

Before hiring team members, identify the specific roles and responsibilities needed to run your SAAS business effectively. This may include positions such as: - Software developers/engineers - UI/UX designers - Data analysts - Customer support representatives - Sales and marketing specialists - Project managers - Quality assurance testers

## Define Desired Skills and Qualifications

Once you have identified the roles, define the desired skills and qualifications for each position. Consider the technical skills, experience, and domain knowledge required to perform the role effectively.

## Recruitment and Hiring

- Utilize various recruitment channels such as online job boards, social media, and professional networks to attract top talent. - Craft job descriptions that accurately represent the roles and responsibilities of each position. - Screen and interview candidates to assess their fit with your organizational culture and values. - Consider using technical assessments and coding challenges to evaluate the technical proficiency of potential team members. - Ensure a diverse and inclusive hiring process by promoting equal opportunities for all candidates.

# Training and Development

Investing in the training and development of your team members is crucial for their growth and the success of your SAAS business. Provide ongoing training opportunities to enhance their skills and knowledge in their respective roles. Regularly evaluate and provide feedback to help them improve their performance.

# Team Collaboration and Communication

Encourage collaboration and effective communication within your team. Foster an environment that promotes teamwork, knowledge sharing, and open communication. Utilize project management tools and collaboration platforms to streamline workflows and facilitate communication.

# Retention and Recognition

Retaining top talent is essential for the long-term success of your SAAS business. Implement strategies to recognize and reward exceptional performance. Offer career growth opportunities, competitive compensation packages, and a positive work environment to create a strong employee retention rate.

## CONCLUSION

Building a strong team is crucial for the success and growth of your SAAS business. By carefully identifying roles and responsibilities, recruiting top talent, providing training and development opportunities, fostering collaboration, and implementing retention strategies, you can build a capable and motivated team that drives your business forward. Remember that hiring the right people and creating a positive work environment will be a valuable investment in the future of your SAAS business.

# Chapter 20: Outsourcing and Freelancing in the No Code SAAS Space

Outsourcing and freelancing have become increasingly popular in the software development industry, and the no code SAAS space is no exception. In this chapter, we will explore how outsourcing and freelancing can benefit your no code SAAS business and provide valuable resources for your development needs.

# THE ADVANTAGES OF OUTSOURCING AND FREELANCING

Outsourcing and freelancing offer several advantages when it comes to building and scaling your no code SAAS application. Here are some key benefits:

## Access to Global Talent

By outsourcing or hiring freelancers, you can tap into a vast pool of global talents. This gives you access to professionals with a wide range of skills and expertise that may not be available locally. With the no code approach, you can work with developers, designers, marketers, and other specialists who are familiar with no code platforms and can help you achieve your development goals.

## Cost-Effectiveness

Outsourcing and freelancing can be cost-effective options compared to hiring a full-time, in-house team. When outsourcing, you can find skilled professionals who offer competitive rates, allowing you to save on expenses such as salaries, benefits, and office space. Freelancers also provide flexibility, as you can hire them on a per-project basis, reducing costs during slower development periods.

# Flexibility and Scalability

Outsourcing and freelancing offer flexibility and scalability for your no code SAAS business. You can easily scale your team up or down based on your current needs. If you have a sudden increase in development requirements, you can quickly hire freelancers or outsource tasks to meet the demand. Conversely, during slower periods, you can reduce the team size or pause outsourcing contracts until needed again.

# Focus on Core Competencies

By outsourcing non-core tasks, you can focus on your core competencies and strategic initiatives. This allows you to allocate more time and resources towards developing and improving your no code SAAS application. Outsourcing tasks like customer support, backend maintenance, or UI/UX design to external experts can save you time and ensure quality in those areas.

# CONSIDERATIONS FOR OUTSOURCING AND FREELANCING

While outsourcing and freelancing can bring numerous benefits, it's important to consider certain factors to ensure smooth collaboration and successful outcomes. Here are some key considerations:

# Clear Communication and Expectations

Establish clear communication channels and expectations with your outsourcing partners or freelancers. Regularly communicate project requirements, deadlines, and deliverables. Use project management tools and collaboration platforms to facilitate communication, track progress, and share files and resources.

# Quality Assurance and Management

Implement quality assurance measures to ensure the outsourced work meets your standards. Define clear guidelines, conduct regular reviews, and provide feedback to ensure the work aligns with your desired outcomes. This may involve performing code reviews, conducting user testing, and monitoring performance metrics to maintain the expected quality of your no code SAAS application.

# Data Security and Confidentiality

When outsourcing, it's crucial to prioritize data security and confidentiality. Ensure that any external partners or freelancers adhere to strict security practices and sign non-disclosure agreements. Implement proper data encryption, access controls, and backup procedures to safeguard your sensitive information and protect user data.

# Managing Multiple Vendors or Freelancers

If you choose to work with multiple outsourcing partners or freelancers, it's important to manage these relationships effectively. Designate a project manager or team lead to coordinate communication and ensure seamless collaboration between all stakeholders. Regularly review and assess the performance of each vendor or freelancer and make necessary adjustments to maintain a productive working relationship.

# CONCLUSION

Outsourcing and freelancing can be valuable resources for your no code SAAS business, providing access to global talent, cost-effectiveness, flexibility, and the ability to focus on your core competencies. With clear communication, quality assurance measures, data security protocols, and effective management, outsourcing and freelancing can help you scale your no code SAAS application and meet customer demands efficiently. Harness the benefits of outsourcing and freelancing to leverage the expertise and skills needed for your no code SAAS success.

# Chapter 21: Legal Considerations for Your SAAS Business

As a software-as-a-service (SAAS) business owner, it's crucial to understand and comply with the legal requirements and considerations that come with operating in the digital space. Failing to address these matters can lead to legal disputes, financial penalties, and damage to your brand reputation. In this chapter, we will explore the key legal considerations that every SAAS entrepreneur should be aware of and provide guidance on how to navigate them.

## UNDERSTANDING INTELLECTUAL PROPERTY RIGHTS

One of the most critical legal aspects of your SAAS business is protecting your intellectual property (IP) rights. This includes any original software code, designs, logos, trademarks, and other creative works that you have developed. Here are a few key points to consider:

## Trademark Registration

Registering your brand name, logo, or slogan as a trademark is essential to prevent others from using similar marks that can cause confusion among consumers. Consult with a trademark attorney to understand the registration process and ensure that your trademarks are adequately protected.

# Copyright Protection

Copyright law automatically grants you ownership of your original creative works. However, it is advisable to register your copyrights with the appropriate authorities to strengthen your legal position in case of infringement disputes.

# Software Licensing

Establish clear licensing terms and conditions for your SAAS application to protect your software from unauthorized use, copying, or distribution. Use comprehensive end-user license agreements (EULAs) that outline the rights and restrictions governing the use of your software.

# DATA PRIVACY AND SECURITY

In today's digital landscape, data privacy and security have become major concerns for businesses and consumers alike. As a SAAS entrepreneur, it is crucial to prioritize data protection and comply with relevant privacy laws, such as the General Data Protection Regulation (GDPR) in the European Union. Here's what you need to consider:

# Privacy Policies

Develop and prominently display a privacy policy that explains how you collect, store, use, and protect user data. Ensure that your policy is clear, transparent, and compliant with applicable data protection laws.

# Data Transfer and Storage

Implement appropriate security measures to protect user data from unauthorized access, such as encryption, access controls, and regular backups. If you transfer user data across international borders, ensure compliance with data transfer regulations, such as the EU-US Privacy Shield or Standard Contractual Clauses.

# User Consent and Opt-Out Mechanisms

Obtain explicit consent from users before collecting their personal information and provide mechanisms for them to opt out of data collection or request the removal of their data.

## CONTRACTUAL AGREEMENTS AND TERMS OF SERVICE

Clear and well-drafted contractual agreements are crucial for establishing the legal relationship between your SAAS business and its customers. Consider the following:

# Terms of Service

Develop comprehensive terms of service that outline the rights and responsibilities of both your company and your customers. Include clauses related to service availability, updates and maintenance, user obligations, limitations of liability, dispute resolution, and termination.

# Service Level Agreements (SLAs)

If you offer service guarantees, define the specific uptime, response times, and performance metrics in SLAs. SLAs provide assurance to your customers and help manage expectations.

# Vendor and Partner Agreements

If you work with third-party vendors or partners, establish clear agreements that outline the terms of the partnership, responsibilities, intellectual property rights, and confidentiality obligations.

# COMPLIANCE WITH INDUSTRY REGULATIONS

Depending on the industry in which your SAAS application operates, there may be specific regulatory requirements that you must comply with. Some common examples include:

# Health Insurance Portability and Accountability Act (HIPAA)

If your SAAS application handles protected health information (PHI), you must comply with strict data privacy and security requirements under HIPAA.

# Payment Card Industry Data Security Standard (PCI DSS)

If you process credit card payments, you need to follow the security standards set by PCI DSS to protect cardholder data.

# Financial Regulations

If your SAAS application involves financial transactions or services, you may need to comply with regulations such as Anti-Money Laundering (AML) and Know Your Customer (KYC) requirements.

# CONCLUSION

Understanding and addressing legal considerations is vital for your SAAS business's success and long-term viability. Consult with legal professionals who specialize in technology and SAAS to ensure that you have proper legal protection, comply with relevant laws, and mitigate any potential legal risks. By proactively addressing these legal considerations, you can build a solid foundation for your

SAAS business and focus on delivering value to your customers without legal hindrances.

# Chapter 22: Customer Support and Success Strategies

Customer support and success are key factors in the long-term success of any SAAS business. Providing exceptional support and ensuring customer success not only helps retain existing customers but also attracts new ones through positive word-of-mouth. In this chapter, we will explore strategies and best practices for effective customer support and success in the no code SAAS industry.

## THE IMPORTANCE OF CUSTOMER SUPPORT AND SUCCESS

Customer support and success play a critical role in the overall success of a SAAS business. Here are some reasons why they are crucial: 1. Retention: Satisfied customers are more likely to continue using your SAAS application, leading to higher customer retention rates. This helps maintain a steady revenue stream and reduces the need for acquiring new customers. 2. Customer Advocacy: Happy customers are more inclined to recommend your SAAS application to others, thereby acting as brand advocates and helping you attract new customers. 3. Reputation:

Providing exceptional customer support and ensuring customer success helps build a positive reputation for your SAAS business. This can lead to increased trust and credibility among potential customers. 4. Upselling and Expansion: Engaging in proactive customer support and ensuring customer success creates opportunities for upselling and expansion. Satisfied customers are more likely to take advantage of additional features or upgrade to higher-priced plans.

# STRATEGIES FOR EFFECTIVE CUSTOMER SUPPORT AND SUCCESS

Implementing effective customer support and success strategies can help differentiate your SAAS business from competitors and drive customer satisfaction. Here are some strategies to consider:

# 1. Proactive Support

Rather than waiting for customers to reach out with issues or concerns, take a proactive approach to customer support. This means actively monitoring customer behavior, gathering feedback, and addressing any potential problems before they escalate. Offer resources such as self-help documentation, knowledge bases, and video tutorials to empower customers to find solutions on their own.

# 2. Prompt and Responsive Communication

Respond to customer inquiries and support tickets in a timely manner. Aim to provide prompt responses, whether it's through email, live chat, or phone support. Make sure your support team is well-trained and equipped with the necessary tools to efficiently address customer concerns.

# 3. Personalization and Customization

Tailor your support approach to meet each customer's specific needs. Take the time to understand their unique requirements and provide personalized recommendations and solutions. This can greatly enhance customer satisfaction and make them feel valued.

# 4. Customer Onboarding and Training

Provide comprehensive onboarding and training resources to help customers get started with your SAAS application. This could include documentation, video tutorials, webinars, or one-on-one training sessions. By ensuring customers have a smooth and successful onboarding experience, you set them up for long-term success.

# 5. Continuous Education and Engagement

Invest in ongoing education and engagement initiatives to help customers maximize the value they get from your SAAS application. This could include hosting webinars, creating a community forum for customers to interact and share best practices, or sending regular newsletters with product updates and tips.

# 6. Customer Success Managers

Consider assigning dedicated customer success managers (CSMs) to key accounts. CSMs can build strong relationships with customers, understand their unique goals and challenges, and provide personalized guidance and support. This personalized attention can significantly impact customer satisfaction and loyalty.

# 7. Gather and Act on Customer Feedback

Regularly gather customer feedback through surveys, feedback forms, or direct conversations. Analyze the feedback to identify areas for improvement or new features and enhancements. Act on this feedback by continuously iterating and improving your SAAS application.

## 8. Measure Customer Success Metrics

Define and track customer success metrics to evaluate the effectiveness of your support strategies. Common metrics include customer satisfaction (CSAT), Net Promoter Score (NPS), churn rate, and renewal rate. Regularly monitor these metrics to identify trends and areas for improvement.

## CONCLUSION

Customer support and success are crucial aspects of running a successful no code SAAS business. By implementing proactive support strategies, ensuring prompt communication, and providing personalized assistance, you can enhance the overall customer experience. Remember to continuously gather customer feedback, measure success metrics, and iterate on your support strategies to ensure long-term customer satisfaction and success.

# Chapter 23: Analyzing Data for Improved SAAS Performance

Data analysis plays a crucial role in improving the performance of SAAS applications. By gathering and analyzing data, SAAS businesses can gain valuable insights into user behavior, application usage patterns, and overall performance metrics. This chapter explores the importance of data analysis and provides strategies for leveraging data to enhance SAAS application performance.

# THE IMPORTANCE OF DATA ANALYSIS

Effective data analysis allows SAAS businesses to make informed decisions and optimize their applications for improved performance. Here are some key reasons why analyzing data is essential:

## 1. Understanding User Behavior:

Data analysis enables SAAS businesses to gain insights into how users interact with their applications. By analyzing user behavior data, such as click-through rates, session duration, and feature usage, businesses can identify patterns and trends. This information helps in making data-driven decisions to enhance user experience, prioritize feature development, and optimize user workflows.

## 2. Identifying Bottlenecks and Performance Issues:

Data analysis helps identify performance bottlenecks, such as slow response times, high error rates, or scalability issues. By monitoring application performance metrics, such as server response time, page load time, and server error rates, businesses can pinpoint performance issues and take necessary actions to resolve them. This leads to improved application performance and user satisfaction.

# 3. Personalization and Customization:

Analyzing user data allows businesses to personalize and tailor their SAAS applications to individual user preferences. By understanding user demographics, usage patterns, and preferences, businesses can offer personalized recommendations, customized features, and targeted marketing campaigns. This enhances user engagement, loyalty, and overall user satisfaction.

# 4. Decision-making and Strategic Planning:

Data analysis provides businesses with solid evidence and insights to drive decision-making and strategic planning. By analyzing key business metrics, such as revenue, customer acquisition costs, churn rates, and customer lifetime value, SAAS businesses can identify growth opportunities, evaluate the success of marketing campaigns, and make data-driven decisions for future planning.

# STRATEGIES FOR LEVERAGING DATA ANALYSIS

To effectively analyze data and improve SAAS performance, businesses can implement the following strategies:

## 1. Define Key Performance Metrics:

Identify the key performance metrics that align with your business goals and objectives. These may include user engagement metrics (such as active users, retention rates, and session duration), conversion rates, revenue growth, customer churn rates, and customer satisfaction scores. Having clear benchmarks and goals will guide your data analysis efforts.

## 2. Implement Analytics Tools:

Leverage analytics tools and platforms to collect and analyze data. Popular analytics tools like Google Analytics, Mixpanel, or Amplitude can provide valuable insights into user behavior, application usage, and performance metrics. These tools offer features for tracking events, user journeys, funnels, and custom metrics. Integrate these tools into your SAAS application to gather the necessary data for analysis.

# 3. Utilize Data Visualization Techniques:

Data visualization techniques, such as charts, graphs, and dashboards, help transform complex data into understandable and actionable insights. Visual representations of data make it easier to identify patterns, trends, and anomalies. Use data visualization tools, such as Tableau or Power BI, to create visually appealing and informative dashboards for better data analysis and reporting.

# 4. Conduct A/B Testing:

A/B testing allows businesses to compare different versions of their SAAS application and measure the impact of changes on user behavior and performance. By running controlled experiments, businesses can analyze the data to determine which version performs better in terms of user engagement, conversion rates, or revenue generation. This data-driven approach helps optimize the application for improved performance.

# 5. Continuously Monitor and Iteratively Improve:

Data analysis should not be a one-time process but a continuous effort. Regularly monitor key performance metrics, analyze user feedback, and gather data to identify areas for improvement. Use A/B testing, user surveys, and feedback loops to gather insights and refine your SAAS application based on user needs and preferences.

Continuously iterate and enhance your application to provide a better user experience.

## CONCLUSION

Analyzing data is crucial for improving the performance of SAAS applications. By understanding user behavior, identifying bottlenecks, personalizing user experiences, and making data-driven decisions, businesses can optimize their SAAS applications for better performance. Implementing data analysis strategies and leveraging analytics tools empowers SAAS businesses to continuously monitor, analyze, and improve their application's performance, leading to increased user satisfaction and business growth.

# Chapter 24: The Role of UX/UI Design in No Code SAAS

When it comes to building successful no code SAAS applications, user experience (UX) and user interface (UI) design play a crucial role. UX/UI design focuses on creating intuitive and user-friendly interfaces that enhance the overall user experience. In this chapter, we will explore the significance of UX/UI design in the context of no code SAAS applications and discuss best practices for creating visually appealing and user-centered designs.

# THE IMPORTANCE OF UX/UI DESIGN IN NO CODE SAAS

Effective UX/UI design is vital for the success of any software application, including no code SAAS. Here are a few reasons why UX/UI design is crucial in the no code SAAS industry: 1. User Satisfaction: A well-designed and user-friendly interface improves user satisfaction by providing a seamless and enjoyable experience. Users are more likely to engage with and continue using a SAAS application that is visually appealing and easy to navigate. 2. Usability and Accessibility: UX/UI design ensures that a no code SAAS application is easy to use and accessible to all users, regardless of their technical background. Intuitive design elements, such as clear navigation bars, interactive buttons, and visual cues, make it easier for users to understand and interact with the application. 3. Brand Identity: UX/UI design plays a significant role in establishing and reflecting the brand identity of a SAAS application. Consistent use of colors, typography, and visual elements that align with the brand's values and target audience helps create a memorable and cohesive user experience. 4. Differentiation and Competitiveness: In a crowded market, a well-designed SAAS application can stand out from the competition. Good UX/UI design can differentiate a product and give it a competitive edge by delivering a unique and delightful user experience.

# BEST PRACTICES FOR UX/UI DESIGN IN NO CODE SAAS

To create an impactful UX/UI design for your no code SAAS application, consider the following best practices: 1. User Research: Understand your target users by conducting user research, including surveys and interviews. Gain insights into their needs, pain points, and preferences. This research will inform your design decisions and help create a user-centered interface. 2. Clear Information Hierarchy: Organize information in a logical and hierarchical manner, making it easy for users to navigate and find what they need. Use clear headings, subheadings, and visual cues to guide users through the application. 3. Consistent Visuals: Maintain consistency in visual elements, such as colors, typography, and icons. Consistency creates a sense of familiarity and improves the user's ability to navigate and understand the application. 4. Responsive Design: Design your SAAS application to be responsive across different devices and screen sizes. Ensure that the interface adapts and displays correctly on mobile devices, tablets, and desktops. 5. Intuitive Navigation: Design a clear and intuitive navigation system that allows users to move effortlessly through the application. Use recognizable icons, logical menu structures, and breadcrumb trails to guide users. 6. Accessibility Considerations: Ensure that your SAAS application is accessible to all users, including those with disabilities. Adhere to web accessibility standards and guidelines to make your application usable by a wider audience. 7. Visual Hierarchy: Use visual hierarchy principles to prioritize and emphasize important elements.

Utilize contrast, size variation, and positioning to draw attention to key information and actions. 8. Feedback and Reassurance: Provide clear and timely feedback to users when they interact with the application. Use loading indicators, progress bars, and success messages to reassure users that their actions are being processed. 9. Iterative Design Process: Adopt an iterative design process that involves continuous feedback and improvement. Use user testing, A/B testing, and analytics to gather data and make informed design decisions. 10. Collaboration with Developers: Work closely with developers to ensure that the design is feasible and can be implemented efficiently within the chosen no code platform. Collaboration between designers and developers is essential for a successful SAAS application. By following these best practices, you can create a visually appealing and user-friendly no code SAAS application that provides an exceptional user experience.

# CONCLUSION

UX/UI design plays a pivotal role in creating successful no code SAAS applications. By prioritizing user satisfaction, usability, brand identity, and differentiation, you can create intuitive and visually appealing interfaces. Incorporating best practices such as user research, clear information hierarchy, responsive design, and collaboration with developers can help you design an exceptional UX/UI for your no code SAAS application. Remember, a well-designed application enhances user engagement, drives customer loyalty, and contributes to the overall success of your SAAS business.

# Chapter 25: Developing API Integrations for Your SAAS Application

In today's interconnected world, the ability to integrate with other applications and services is crucial for the success of a software-as-a-service (SAAS) application. Developing API integrations allows your SAAS application to connect and exchange data with third-party systems, providing enhanced functionality and value to your users.

## UNDERSTANDING API INTEGRATION

An Application Programming Interface (API) acts as an interface that enables different software systems to communicate and interact with each other. API integrations allow your SAAS application to leverage the capabilities of other systems, such as payment gateways, CRM platforms, email marketing services, and more. API integrations enable data exchange, functionality sharing, and seamless collaboration between applications. By integrating with popular platforms, you can extend the capabilities of your SAAS application and provide a more comprehensive solution to your users.

# BENEFITS OF API INTEGRATIONS

Developing API integrations for your SAAS application brings numerous benefits, including:

## Expanded Functionality:

API integrations allow you to leverage the features and functionalities of other applications, thereby expanding the capabilities of your SAAS application. This enables you to offer a more comprehensive solution to your users without developing those functionalities from scratch.

## Improved User Experience:

Integrating with popular platforms or services that your users are already familiar with can enhance their overall user experience. For example, by integrating with a popular CRM platform, you can seamlessly sync data between the two systems, providing a smooth and efficient user experience.

## Streamlined Workflows:

API integrations automate data exchange between different systems, eliminating the need for manual data entry or repetitive tasks. This streamlines workflows and increases operational efficiency, allowing your users to focus on more important tasks.

# Scalability and Flexibility:

API integrations enable your SAAS application to scale and adapt to changing business requirements. As your users' needs evolve, you can easily integrate with new systems or services to provide additional value and keep up with market demands.

# Competitive Advantage:

By offering API integrations with popular platforms, your SAAS application stands out from competitors who may not have the same level of integration capabilities. This can give you a competitive edge in the market and attract more users to your application.

## DEVELOPING API INTEGRATIONS

Developing API integrations for your SAAS application involves several key steps:

# Identify Integration Opportunities:

Determine which platforms or services will provide the most value to your users when integrated with your SAAS application. Conduct market research and gather user feedback to identify the key integration opportunities that align with your users' needs and preferences.

# Understand API Documentation:

Carefully review the API documentation provided by the platforms or services you plan to integrate with. Understand the endpoints, authentication methods, data formats, rate limits, and any other requirements for making successful API requests.

## Plan Integration Workflow:

Map out the flow of data and functionalities between your SAAS application and the integrated system. Define how data will be exchanged, what triggers certain actions, and how error handling and fallback mechanisms will be implemented.

## Develop Integration Code:

Utilize the programming languages and frameworks supported by the integrated systems to develop the integration code. Use the provided SDKs, libraries, or wrappers to simplify the integration process and ensure compatibility and reliability.

## Test and Debug:

Thoroughly test the integration to ensure that it functions as expected. Simulate different scenarios, handle edge cases, and debug any issues that arise during the testing phase. Prioritize the security and stability of the integration.

# Document Integration:

Create clear and concise documentation for your API integration, detailing the endpoints, data structures, authentication requirements, and any limitations or considerations. This documentation will help users understand and utilize the integration effectively.

# Monitor and Maintain:

Regularly monitor the performance and reliability of your API integrations. Stay updated with any changes or updates from the integrated platforms and adapt your integration code accordingly. Address any issues or bugs promptly to ensure a seamless experience for your users.

# CONCLUSION

Developing API integrations for your SAAS application opens up new avenues for functionality, scalability, and user satisfaction. By strategically integrating with other platforms and services, you can provide a more comprehensive solution to your users, streamline workflows, and stay competitive in the market. Invest in developing robust API integrations to unlock the full potential of your SAAS application.

# Chapter 26: Securing Your SAAS Application and User Data

## IMPORTANCE OF SECURING YOUR SAAS APPLICATION AND USER DATA

In an era where data breaches and cyber threats are increasingly common, securing your SAAS application and user data is of utmost importance. As a SAAS entrepreneur, it is your responsibility to ensure that your application and the sensitive information it handles are protected from unauthorized access, data breaches, and other security risks. By implementing robust security measures, you can gain the trust of your customers and safeguard their valuable data.

## UNDERSTANDING THE RISKS

Before diving into the security measures, it is essential to understand the potential risks and vulnerabilities that your SAAS application and user data may face. Some common risks include: 1. Unauthorized access: Hackers may attempt to gain unauthorized access to your application and user data by exploiting vulnerabilities in your system. 2. Data breaches: Data breaches can occur when sensitive user information, such as names, email addresses, passwords, or payment details, are accessed, stolen, or exposed without permission. 3. Denial-of-Service (DoS) attacks: DoS attacks aim to overload your application servers, making them unavailable to legitimate users. 4. Cross-Site Scripting (XSS) attacks: XSS attacks involve injecting malicious scripts into your application, potentially allowing attackers to steal user data or hijack user sessions. 5. SQL injection attacks: SQL injection attacks exploit vulnerabilities in your application's database queries to gain unauthorized access or perform malicious actions. 6. Insecure APIs: If your SAAS application utilizes APIs, vulnerabilities in these interfaces can be exploited to compromise data or gain unauthorized access.

# IMPLEMENTING SECURITY MEASURES

To protect your SAAS application and user data, consider implementing the following security measures: 1. Secure coding practices: Adhere to secure coding practices, such as input validation, parameterized queries, and secure encryption algorithms, to prevent common vulnerabilities like XSS and SQL injection attacks. 2. Access control: Implement robust authentication and authorization mechanisms to ensure that only authorized users can access sensitive functionalities and data. 3. Encryption: Use encryption techniques, such as HTTPS/TLS, to secure data transmission between your application and users' devices. 4. Regular updates and patches: Keep your SAAS application and underlying infrastructure up to date with the latest security patches and updates to address potential vulnerabilities. 5. Security testing and vulnerability assessments: Conduct regular security testing, including penetration testing and vulnerability assessments, to identify and address any weaknesses or vulnerabilities in your system. 6. Data backups and disaster recovery: Establish regular data backup procedures and implement a disaster recovery plan to ensure that you can quickly restore operations in the event of a security incident or system failure. 7. Real-time monitoring and intrusion detection: Implement intrusion detection systems and real-time monitoring to identify and respond to any suspicious activities or security breaches promptly. 8. Employee training: Educate your employees about security best practices, including password hygiene, phishing awareness, and proper handling of sensitive data. 9. Privacy policies and user consent: Clearly define and communicate your privacy policies to users, ensuring that they understand how their data will be collected, used, and protected.

# COMPLIANCE AND REGULATIONS

Compliance with relevant regulations and industry standards is essential to ensure data security in your SAAS application. Some common regulations to consider include: 1. General Data Protection Regulation (GDPR): If you handle personal data of European Union residents, ensure compliance with GDPR requirements, including data protection, user consent, and breach notification obligations. 2. Payment Card Industry Data Security

Standard (PCI DSS): If your SAAS application processes payment card transactions, comply with PCI DSS requirements to secure cardholder data and maintain a secure payment environment. 3. Health Insurance Portability and Accountability Act (HIPAA): If your SAAS application handles protected health information (PHI), ensure that you meet HIPAA requirements for data privacy and security in the healthcare industry.

## CONCLUSION

Securing your SAAS application and user data is crucial for building customer trust, maintaining data privacy, and safeguarding against security breaches. By implementing robust security measures, staying compliant with regulations, and regularly updating your security practices, you can protect your SAAS application and user data from potential threats, ensuring the long-term success of your business. Remember, security should be an ongoing effort to adapt and respond to evolving cybersecurity risks.

# Chapter 28: Case Study: From No Code to SAAS Millionaire

In this chapter, we will explore a real-life case study of an individual who successfully transitioned from a no code developer to a SAAS millionaire. This case study will provide valuable insights into the journey, challenges, and strategies employed to achieve such financial success in the no code SAAS industry.

# CASE STUDY: JOHN'S ENTREPRENEURIAL JOURNEY

**Background:** John, a creative and ambitious individual with no prior coding experience, discovered the power of no code platforms and saw an opportunity to create innovative SAAS applications without relying on traditional coding skills. With this newfound motivation, John embarked on his entrepreneurial journey. **Identifying a Problem:** John started by identifying a common problem faced by businesses and individuals, which could be solved through a SAAS application. He conducted thorough market research, analyzed competitors, and spoke to potential users to validate the demand for his solution. **Building the SAAS Application:** Using a no code platform, John began developing his SAAS application. He leveraged drag-and-drop functionalities, pre-built templates, and ready-to-use components to create a visually appealing and user-friendly interface. **Iterative Development:** John adopted an iterative development approach, continuously refining and improving his application based on user feedback. He actively sought user feedback, implemented necessary changes, and closely monitored usage patterns to ensure customer satisfaction. **Marketing and User Acquisition:** John developed a comprehensive marketing strategy to promote his SAAS application. He utilized content marketing to educate and engage his target audience, leveraged social media platforms to reach a wider audience, and collaborated with influencers to generate buzz and credibility. Through effective marketing efforts, John successfully acquired a significant user base. **Monetization:** John employed a subscription-based pricing model for his SAAS application, offering different pricing tiers to cater to a range of customer needs and budgets. Additionally, he implemented upselling strategies to generate extra revenue by offering premium features and add-ons. **Customer Support and Success:** Understanding the importance of customer satisfaction, John prioritized top-notch customer support. He provided timely assistance, proactively addressed customer concerns, and ensured seamless onboarding and product training. By focusing on customer success, John cultivated a loyal customer base and received positive word-of-mouth recommendations. **Scaling and Expansion:** As his SAAS business flourished, John focused on scaling and expanding his operations. He recruited a talented team to support business growth, optimized infrastructure to handle increased application usage, and continued to innovate and add new features to stay ahead of the competition. **Continuous Learning and Improvement:** Throughout the journey, John maintained a mindset of continuous learning and improvement. He stayed updated with industry trends, sought inspiration from successful SAAS entrepreneurs, attended relevant conferences and events, and adapted his strategies to align with changing market demands. **Achieving SAAS Millionaire Status:** Through his dedicated efforts, strategic planning, and relentless pursuit of excellence, John's SAAS application achieved remarkable success. The revenue generated from subscriptions, upsells, and partnerships propelled him to the coveted SAAS millionaire status.

# KEY TAKEAWAYS

- Identifying a problem and understanding market demand is crucial for success in the no code SAAS industry. - Building a visually appealing and user-friendly SAAS application using no code platforms can level the playing field for individuals without coding experience. - Continuous improvement based on user feedback leads to a better product and higher customer satisfaction. - A well-rounded marketing strategy helps in acquiring a substantial user base. - Implementing effective monetization strategies, such as subscription-based pricing and upselling, contributes to financial success. - Prioritizing customer support and success maintains customer loyalty and drives positive word-of-mouth recommendations. - Scaling and expansion require careful planning, investment in infrastructure, and continuous innovation. - Continuous learning, adaptation, and staying abreast of industry trends are vital for long-term success in the no code SAAS industry. **Conclusion:** The case study of John's journey from no code to SAAS millionaire provides invaluable insights and inspiration for aspiring entrepreneurs in the no code SAAS industry. By leveraging the power of no code platforms, embracing continuous improvement, and implementing effective strategies, individuals can achieve remarkable success and financial freedom in this rapidly growing industry.

# Chapter 29: Tips for Building a Profitable SAAS Marketplace

Building a profitable software-as-a-service (SAAS) marketplace requires careful planning, strategic decision-making, and a deep understanding of the needs and preferences of both the buyers and sellers in your target market. In this chapter, we'll explore some key tips and strategies that can help you build a successful and profitable SAAS marketplace.

## 1. IDENTIFY A NICHE MARKET

When building a SAAS marketplace, it's important to focus on a specific niche market that has a clear demand for your product or service. By identifying a niche market, you can tailor your offering to meet the specific needs of your target customers, making it easier to attract and retain users. Conduct thorough market research to identify untapped opportunities and validate the demand for your marketplace.

## 2. BUILD A USER-FRIENDLY INTERFACE

A user-friendly interface is crucial for attracting and retaining users on your SAAS marketplace. Invest in intuitive design and navigation to ensure that users can easily navigate through your platform, search for products or services, and complete transactions. Consider implementing features such as filters, search bars, and personalized recommendations to enhance the user experience and help users find what they need quickly.

## 3. IMPLEMENT SECURE PAYMENT SYSTEMS

Building trust is essential for a profitable SAAS marketplace. Implement secure and reliable payment systems to safeguard user transactions and protect sensitive information. Offer multiple payment options and ensure that these systems comply with industry standards and regulations. Building a reputation for secure transactions will not only attract more buyers but also encourage sellers to join your marketplace.

## 4. PROVIDE EFFICIENT CUSTOMER SUPPORT

Efficient customer support is crucial for building a profitable SAAS marketplace. Offer multiple channels for users to reach out for assistance, such as email, live chat, or a dedicated support center. Ensure that your support team is responsive and knowledgeable, addressing user concerns in a timely manner. By providing excellent customer support, you can enhance user satisfaction and build a loyal customer base.

# 5. IMPLEMENT EFFECTIVE MARKETING STRATEGIES

Marketing plays a vital role in driving user acquisition and generating revenue for your SAAS marketplace. Implement effective marketing strategies to increase awareness and attract users to your platform. Leverage various channels such as social media, content marketing, paid advertising, and influencer partnerships to reach your target audience. Create engaging content that highlights the unique value proposition of your marketplace and showcases the benefits of using your platform.

# 6. FOSTER TRUST AND SAFETY

Building trust and ensuring the safety of users' data and transactions is key to building a profitable SAAS marketplace. Implement measures to verify the identity of sellers and buyers, such as user authentication or verification processes. Establish clear terms and policies to protect users from fraud or misconduct. Regularly monitor and moderate the marketplace to ensure compliance with your terms of service and maintain a safe environment for all users.

# 7. ENCOURAGE USER ENGAGEMENT

User engagement is directly linked to the profitability of your SAAS marketplace. Implement features that encourage user participation and interaction, such as reviews and ratings, social sharing, and community forums. Foster a sense of community and provide incentives for users to engage with your platform, such as loyalty programs or rewards for referrals. Increased user engagement leads to higher customer satisfaction and can drive increased usage and revenue.

# 8. CONTINUOUSLY IMPROVE AND INNOVATE

To stay competitive and profitable in the SAAS marketplace industry, it's important to continuously improve and innovate your platform. Regularly collect user feedback and analyze data to identify areas for improvement. Stay updated with industry trends and evolving user needs to ensure that your marketplace remains relevant and attractive to both buyers and sellers. Embrace innovation and be open to exploring new features or partnerships that can enhance the value of your SAAS marketplace. In conclusion, building a profitable SAAS marketplace requires a combination of strategic planning, user-centric design, efficient customer support, effective marketing, trust and safety measures, user engagement, and continuous improvement. By implementing these tips and strategies, you can position your SAAS marketplace for success and drive profitability in the long run.

# Chapter 30: Building Custom Extensions for SAAS Applications

Extensions play a vital role in expanding the functionality and customization options of SAAS applications. They allow users to tailor the application to their specific needs and enhance their overall experience. In this chapter, we will explore the process of building custom extensions for SAAS applications and the benefits they offer.

## UNDERSTANDING THE IMPORTANCE OF CUSTOM EXTENSIONS

SAAS applications are designed to provide a wide range of features and functionalities that cater to the needs of various users. However, every user has unique requirements, and there may be instances where the standard features of the SAAS application do not fully meet their needs. This is where custom extensions come into play. Custom extensions enable users to extend the functionality of the SAAS application and integrate additional features that are specific to their business process. Whether it's integrating with third-party services, adding new functionality, or enhancing existing features, custom extensions empower users to customize the SAAS application according to their requirements.

# THE BENEFITS OF BUILDING CUSTOM EXTENSIONS

Building custom extensions for SAAS applications offers several benefits for both the SAAS provider and the end-users: 1. **Increased Flexibility:** Custom extensions provide users with the flexibility to tailor the SAAS application to their specific needs. This ensures that they can perform tasks efficiently and effectively. 2. **Enhanced User Experience:** When users can customize the SAAS application with custom extensions, they can streamline their workflows and optimize their productivity. This leads to an improved user experience. 3. **Competitive Advantage:** Custom extensions allow SAAS providers to differentiate their offering from competitors. The ability to provide additional functionality through custom extensions can attract more users and create a competitive edge. 4. **Scalability:** Custom extensions enable SAAS applications to scale and adapt to the evolving needs of users. New features and functionalities can be seamlessly added through custom extensions, ensuring that the application remains relevant. 5. **Revenue Generation:** SAAS providers can leverage custom extensions as an additional revenue stream. By offering premium or specialized extensions, they can monetize the customization capabilities and generate more revenue.

# BUILDING CUSTOM EXTENSIONS FOR SAAS APPLICATIONS

The process of building custom extensions for SAAS applications involves several steps: 1. **Identify User Needs:** Understand the specific requirements and pain points of your target users. Conduct surveys and gather feedback to identify the features and functionalities that would add value to their experience. 2. **Plan the Extension:** Define the scope and requirements of the custom extension. Determine the goals, objectives, and desired outcomes. This will guide the development process and ensure an effective and efficient solution. 3. **Choose the Right Technology:** Select the appropriate technology stack to build the custom extension. Consider factors such as compatibility with the existing SAAS application, scalability, and ease of maintenance. 4. **Develop the Extension:** Utilize the chosen technology stack to develop the custom extension. Follow best practices and coding standards to ensure a robust and secure solution. Test the extension thoroughly to identify and fix any issues. 5. **Integrate the Extension:** Integrate the custom extension seamlessly with the SAAS application. This involves ensuring compatibility, maintaining user interface consistency, and minimizing disruptions to the existing user experience. 6. **Provide Documentation and Support:** Create comprehensive documentation that guides users on how to install, configure, and utilize the custom extension. Offer support channels, such as a help center or chat support, to assist users in resolving any issues they may encounter. 7. **Continuously Improve and Update:** Regularly gather user feedback and analyze usage data to identify areas of improvement. Update the custom extension to address user needs and implement new features or enhancements.

## CONCLUSION

Custom extensions allow users to personalize and enhance their SAAS experience by extending the functionality of the application to meet their unique requirements. By building custom extensions, SAAS providers can offer added value to their users, differentiate themselves from competitors, and generate additional revenue. The process of building custom extensions involves understanding user needs, planning, development, integration, documentation, and continuous improvement. Embracing custom extensions can significantly enhance the overall effectiveness and user satisfaction of SAAS applications.

# Chapter 31: Leveraging Analytics to Drive Revenue

Analytics play a crucial role in driving revenue for SAAS applications. By effectively leveraging analytics, businesses can gain valuable insights into user behavior, identify trends, make data-driven decisions, and optimize their revenue generation strategies. In this chapter, we will explore the importance of analytics in driving revenue and discuss strategies to effectively utilize analytics in your SAAS business.

# UNDERSTANDING THE IMPORTANCE OF ANALYTICS

Analytics provide businesses with valuable information about their customers, products, and overall performance. By analyzing user data, businesses can gain insights that help them understand their customers' needs and preferences, and optimize their revenue generation strategies. Here are some key reasons why analytics are important for driving revenue:

## 1. Customer Behavior Analysis:

Analytics enable businesses to track and analyze customer behavior, from the initial acquisition to the conversion and retention stages. By understanding how customers interact with your SAAS application, you can identify areas for improvement, optimize user journeys, and increase conversions.

## 2. Identify Revenue Opportunities:

Analytics provide insights into customer preferences, buying patterns, and user-generated data. By analyzing this information, businesses can identify new revenue opportunities, such as product upgrades, cross-selling, or introducing new features or pricing models.

# 3. Optimize Pricing and Packaging:

Analyzing data on customer behavior and purchase patterns can help businesses optimize their pricing and packaging strategies. By understanding which pricing tiers or features drive the most revenue, businesses can make informed decisions and tailor their offerings to maximize revenue whilst remaining competitive.

# 4. Churn Prediction and Reduction:

Analytics can help identify customers who are at risk of churning. By analyzing usage patterns, customer interactions, and other relevant data, businesses can proactively address potential issues and develop retention strategies to reduce churn rates and retain valuable customers.

# 5. Performance and Optimization:

Analytics enable businesses to track the performance of their SAAS application and identify areas for improvement. By analyzing metrics such as user engagement, conversion rates, and customer satisfaction, businesses can optimize their product, enhance user experience, and ultimately drive revenue growth.

# STRATEGIES FOR LEVERAGING ANALYTICS TO DRIVE REVENUE

To effectively leverage analytics for revenue generation, businesses should implement the following strategies:

## 1. Define Key Performance Indicators (KPIs):

Identify the key metrics that align with your revenue goals. Examples include customer acquisition cost (CAC), lifetime value (LTV), conversion rates, churn rate, and average revenue per user (ARPU). By regularly tracking these KPIs, you can gain insights into your revenue performance and make data-driven decisions.

## 2. Utilize Advanced Analytics Tools:

Invest in advanced analytics tools that provide in-depth insights, such as cohort analysis, funnel analysis, and predictive analytics. These tools can help you understand user behavior, identify patterns, and make data-driven decisions to optimize revenue generation.

# 3. Implement A/B Testing:

A/B testing allows you to test different variations of your SAAS application or marketing strategies to identify what drives higher revenue. By analyzing the results of A/B tests, you can optimize your offerings, pricing, or marketing strategies accordingly.

# 4. Personalization and Upselling:

Utilize analytics to personalize your offerings and upsell to existing customers. By analyzing user data and preferences, you can deliver targeted product recommendations, promotions, or pricing options to drive additional revenue.

# 5. Cohort Analysis and Customer Segmentation:

Segment your customers based on key characteristics or behaviors. Analyzing cohorts and customer segments can help you identify the most valuable customer groups and tailor your marketing and retention strategies to maximize revenue.

# 6. Predictive Analytics:

Leverage predictive analytics to forecast customer behavior, demand, and revenue. By analyzing historical data and trends, you can make accurate predictions and adjust your strategies to maximize revenue opportunities.

## 7. Implement Data-Driven Decision-Making:

Utilize analytics to drive data-driven decision-making across your organization. By regularly analyzing and sharing insights with your teams, you can align strategies, identify revenue opportunities, and optimize business processes to drive overall revenue growth.

## IN CONCLUSION

Leveraging analytics is crucial for driving revenue in the SAAS industry. By understanding customer behavior, optimizing pricing strategies, reducing churn, and making data-driven decisions, businesses can maximize revenue opportunities and achieve long-term success. Implementing an analytics-driven approach and utilizing advanced analytics tools will allow your SAAS business to stay competitive, agile, and focused on revenue growth.

# Chapter 32: The Future of No Code SAAS

The future of the no code SAAS industry is filled with exciting possibilities and advancements that will continue to revolutionize the way software applications are developed and deployed. As technology evolves and customer demands change, the no code SAAS landscape is expected to undergo significant transformations. In this chapter, we will explore some of the key trends and predictions for the future of no code SAAS.

# RISE OF AI AND AUTOMATION

One of the most significant trends that will shape the future of no code SAAS is the increased integration of artificial intelligence (AI) and automation. AI-powered no code platforms are already making waves by enabling users to create applications with advanced capabilities such as natural language processing, image recognition, and machine learning. These platforms allow individuals and businesses to build intelligent applications without any coding knowledge, further democratizing the software development process. Automation will also play a vital role in the future of no code SAAS. As businesses strive for efficiency and scalability, automation will become increasingly important in streamlining workflows, reducing manual tasks, and improving overall productivity. No code platforms will continue to enhance their automation capabilities, enabling users to automate complex processes with ease.

# INTEGRATION WITH EMERGING TECHNOLOGIES

No code SAAS applications will increasingly leverage emerging technologies to provide even more robust and innovative solutions. Integration with technologies such as virtual reality (VR), augmented reality (AR), blockchain, and Internet of Things (IoT) will open up new possibilities for creating unique and immersive user experiences. For example, no code SAAS platforms may offer drag-and-drop features for building VR and AR applications, allowing users to create virtual experiences without any coding. Integration with blockchain technology will enable the development of secure and decentralized applications, offering increased transparency and data integrity. The integration of IoT will enable the creation of smart applications that can interact with connected devices and gather real-time data.

# ENHANCED COLLABORATION AND CO-CREATION

Collaboration and co-creation will continue to be integral parts of the no code SAAS industry. As no code platforms become more user-friendly and accessible, collaboration among non-technical users, designers, and developers will increase. No code SAAS applications will offer built-in collaboration tools that allow teams to work together in real-time, making it easier to share ideas, iterate on designs, and improve overall application development. Co-creation will also become more prevalent in the no code SAAS space. As users gain more autonomy and control over the development process, they will have the opportunity to contribute to the creation of new features and functionalities. No code SAAS platforms may introduce features that allow users to submit their ideas for improvement or vote on proposed enhancements, creating a collaborative environment that empowers users to shape the direction of the platform.

# ADVANCED CUSTOMIZATION AND PERSONALIZATION

No code SAAS applications of the future will provide even more advanced customization and personalization options. Users will have the ability to tailor every aspect of their applications to meet their specific needs and preferences. Drag-and-drop interfaces will become more intuitive and versatile, allowing for easy customization of user interfaces, workflows, and data structures. Personalization will extend beyond just the visual aspects of the application. No code SAAS platforms will offer machine learning capabilities that enable the application to learn from user interactions and provide personalized recommendations and experiences. This level of personalization will enhance user engagement and satisfaction, ultimately leading to increased customer loyalty and retention.

# THE EVOLVING ROLE OF NO CODE DEVELOPERS

As the no code SAAS industry continues to evolve, the role of no code developers will also change. No code development will become a core competency for many professionals, and a new generation of creators will emerge. No code developers will focus on designing user experiences, customizing workflows, and leveraging automation to build innovative applications. Furthermore, the line between traditional coding and no code development will blur. Traditional developers will also embrace no code platforms as tools to accelerate their development process and create prototypes quickly. The distinction between coding and no code development will become less significant as both approaches converge to create powerful and flexible applications.

# CONCLUSION

The future of no code SAAS is bright and promising. Advancements in AI, automation, collaboration, customization, and personalization will continue to shape the industry. As technology continues to evolve, no code SAAS platforms will empower individuals and businesses to build sophisticated and intelligent applications without the need for coding expertise. The role of no code developers will grow in importance, and the boundaries between coding and no code development will become more fluid. The future of no code SAAS is fueled by innovation, creativity, and the democratization of software development.

# CHAPTER 33: PERSONAL BRANDING AND THOUGHT LEADERSHIP IN THE SAAS SPACE

In the competitive SAAS industry, personal branding and thought leadership are becoming increasingly important for entrepreneurs and professionals to stand out from the crowd and establish themselves as industry experts. Personal branding allows individuals to cultivate their unique identity, showcase their expertise, and build trust with their target audience. Thought leadership, on the other hand, involves sharing valuable insights and knowledge that contributes to the industry's overall growth and development.

# The Power of Personal Branding

Personal branding is about creating a strong and authentic identity that resonates with your target audience. It encompasses various elements, including your reputation, values, expertise, and online presence. Building a personal brand in the SAAS space can offer several benefits: 1. **Establishing Credibility:** A well-defined personal brand can position you as an authority in your field. By consistently sharing valuable content, engaging with your audience, and showcasing your expertise, you can establish yourself as a credible source of information. 2. **Building Trust:** Personal branding humanizes your professional image and helps build trust with your audience. By sharing your story, values, and experiences, you can create a deeper connection with your target market. 3. **Creating Differentiation:** With the SAAS industry becoming increasingly crowded, personal branding can help you stand out from the competition. By showcasing your unique perspectives, skills, and expertise, you can differentiate yourself and attract a loyal following. 4. **Expanding Opportunities:** A strong personal brand can open doors to new opportunities, such as speaking engagements, partnerships, and collaborations. It can also attract potential clients, investors, and job offers.

# Developing Thought Leadership

Thought leadership involves sharing valuable insights, knowledge, and opinions that contribute to the industry's growth and development. It positions you as a trusted advisor and someone at the forefront of innovation and industry trends. Here are some strategies to develop thought leadership in the SAAS space: 1. **Stay Informed:** Keep up with the latest trends, technologies, and industry news. Read books, attend conferences, participate in webinars, and engage in continuous learning to stay up to date. 2. **Create Valuable Content:** Develop a content strategy that aligns with your personal brand and target audience. Write informative blog posts, publish whitepapers or e-books, create video tutorials, or start a podcast. Focus on providing valuable insights, practical tips, and actionable advice. 3. **Speak at Industry Events:** Offer to speak at conferences, webinars, and industry events to showcase your expertise and share your knowledge with a wider audience. Speaking engagements can help you establish yourself as a thought leader and expand your network. 4. **Contribute to Industry Publications:** Write guest articles or contribute insights to prominent industry publications. This can help you reach a larger audience and position yourself as an expert in your field. 5. **Engage in Thoughtful Discussions:** Participate in online communities, forums, and social media groups relevant to the SAAS industry. Engage in conversations, share your insights, and offer help to others. Building relationships and engaging in meaningful discussions can further establish your thought leadership. 6. **Collaborate with Others:** Seek out opportunities to collaborate with other thought leaders in the SAAS space. Co-author blog posts, host joint webinars, or participate in panel discussions. Collaborating with respected professionals can enhance your credibility and extend your reach.

# Benefits of Personal Branding and Thought Leadership in SAAS

Establishing a personal brand and thought leadership in the SAAS space can have several advantages, including: 1. **Attracting Customers:** A strong personal brand and thought leadership can attract potential customers who appreciate your expertise and trust your insights. It can also help foster brand loyalty and repeat business. 2. **Creating Networking Opportunities:** Personal branding and thought leadership can lead to valuable connections and networking opportunities within the SAAS industry. This can open doors to new collaborations, partnerships, and mentorships. 3. **Enhancing Career Growth:** By positioning yourself as a thought leader, you can increase your professional visibility and improve your career prospects. Employers and recruiters are often drawn to professionals who have established a strong personal brand and demonstrated thought leadership. 4. **Driving Industry Innovation:** Thought leaders often play a critical role in driving industry innovation. By sharing your insights and challenging the status quo, you can contribute to the advancement of the SAAS industry as a whole. 5. **Building a Lasting Legacy:** Personal branding and thought leadership allow you to leave a lasting impact on the SAAS industry. By sharing your knowledge and contributing to the growth of the field, you can leave a legacy that inspires and influences future generations.

# Conclusion

In the competitive SAAS industry, personal branding and thought leadership are powerful tools for standing out, establishing credibility, and driving success. By carefully crafting your personal brand, engaging in thoughtful discussions, creating valuable content, and positioning yourself as a trusted advisor, you can attract customers, create networking opportunities, and drive industry innovation. Embrace the power of personal branding and thought leadership to unlock your full potential in the SAAS space.

# Chapter 34: Mental Strategies for Success as a SAAS Entrepreneur

As a SAAS entrepreneur, having the right mindset and mental strategies is essential for navigating the challenges and achieving success in the industry. Building a SAAS business requires perseverance, resilience, and the ability to adapt to changes. In this chapter, we will explore some key mental strategies that can help you thrive as a SAAS entrepreneur.

## 1. EMBRACE A GROWTH MINDSET

One of the fundamental mental strategies for success as a SAAS entrepreneur is to adopt a growth mindset. A growth mindset is the belief that your abilities and intelligence can be developed and improved through dedication and hard work. With a growth mindset, you view challenges as opportunities for growth and learning. Instead of being discouraged by setbacks or failures, you see them as valuable lessons that propel you forward. By embracing a growth mindset, you are more likely to take risks, experiment with new ideas, and continuously seek improvement. Remember that building a SAAS business is a journey filled with ups and downs, and having a growth mindset will help you stay motivated and persistent during challenging times.

# 2. STAY RESILIENT

Resilience is a key trait for success in any entrepreneurial endeavor. As a SAAS entrepreneur, you will inevitably encounter obstacles, setbacks, and even failures. It is crucial to develop resilience, which is the ability to bounce back from adversity and keep moving forward. To cultivate resilience, focus on developing a strong support system. Surround yourself with mentors, fellow entrepreneurs, and industry professionals who can provide guidance, support, and encouragement during difficult times. Take care of your physical and mental well-being by incorporating self-care practices like exercise, meditation, and downtime into your routine. Celebrate small victories along the way to boost your morale and maintain a positive mindset.

# 3. FOSTER A PROBLEM-SOLVING ATTITUDE

As a SAAS entrepreneur, you will face numerous challenges, from technical issues to customer demands. Developing a problem-solving attitude is essential to overcome these obstacles and find effective solutions. Instead of viewing challenges as roadblocks, see them as opportunities to innovate and improve your SAAS application. Approach problems with a systematic and analytical mindset. Break down complex issues into smaller, manageable tasks. Seek creative solutions by thinking outside the box and collaborating with your team. Embrace experimentation and be open to pivoting when necessary. By fostering a problem-solving attitude, you will be better equipped to tackle challenges and find success in the SAAS industry.

# 4. CULTIVATE STRONG COMMUNICATION SKILLS

Effective communication is crucial for success as a SAAS entrepreneur. As you build your business, you will need to communicate with team members, investors, partners, and most importantly, your customers. Clear and concise communication helps build trust, resolve conflicts, and foster strong relationships. Practice active listening to truly understand the needs and concerns of your stakeholders. Develop the ability to translate complex technical concepts into simple and understandable language for your customers. Clearly articulate your vision, goals, and expectations to your team. Build strong relationships with your customers by actively seeking and responding to their feedback.

# 5. MAINTAIN A POSITIVE AND PERSISTENT ATTITUDE

In the fast-paced SAAS industry, maintaining a positive and persistent attitude is vital. There will be times when you face rejection, experience slow growth, or encounter unforeseen challenges. However, it is crucial to remain optimistic and persistently work towards your goals. Celebrate your successes, no matter how small, to maintain a positive mindset. Surround yourself with positive and supportive individuals who believe in your vision. Develop a strong sense of self-motivation and discipline to stay focused on your long-term objectives. Remember, success in the SAAS industry is a marathon, not a sprint. Stay committed, stay positive, and stay persistent.

# CONCLUSION

Developing a strong mental foundation is crucial for success as a SAAS entrepreneur. Embrace a growth mindset, cultivate resilience, foster a problem-solving attitude, develop strong communication skills, and maintain a positive and persistent attitude. By adopting these mental strategies, you will be better equipped to navigate the challenges, capitalize on opportunities, and achieve success in the competitive SAAS industry.

# Chapter 35: Nurturing Partnerships and Collaborations

In the competitive landscape of the no code SAAS industry, nurturing partnerships and collaborations can be a game-changer for your business. By forming strategic alliances with other organizations and individuals, you can leverage their expertise, resources, and network to accelerate your growth and expand your reach. This chapter explores the importance of nurturing partnerships and collaborations and provides strategies for establishing and maintaining successful relationships.

## THE POWER OF PARTNERSHIPS

Partnerships offer numerous benefits for no code SAAS entrepreneurs. Here are a few compelling reasons why nurturing partnerships should be a key focus for your business: 1. Expanded Reach: Collaborating with partners allows you to tap into their existing customer base, increasing your visibility and potentially attracting new users to your SAAS application. 2. Complementary Resources and Expertise: Partnerships enable you to leverage the strengths and expertise of your collaborators. By joining forces, you can benefit from shared knowledge, resources, and technology that can enhance your product offerings and add value to your customers. 3. Enhanced Innovation: Collaborating with other organizations brings fresh perspectives and ideas to the table. By pooling your resources and brainstorming together, you can come up with innovative solutions and create cutting-edge products that address market needs. 4. Access to New Markets: Forming partnerships with organizations operating in different geographic regions or target markets can help you expand your market reach. By leveraging their local knowledge and networks, you can establish a foothold in new territories and gain access to a broader customer base. 5. Risk Mitigation: Partnerships provide an opportunity to share risks and responsibilities. By diversifying your partnerships, you can distribute potential risks and minimize the impact of any setbacks on your business.

# STRATEGIES FOR NURTURING PARTNERSHIPS AND COLLABORATIONS

While partnerships can offer significant advantages, building and maintaining successful collaborations requires careful planning and execution. Here are some strategies to help you nurture partnerships and establish fruitful collaborations: 1. Identify Strategic Partners: The first step is to identify potential partners who align with your business goals and can provide complementary resources or expertise. Look for organizations or individuals that share a similar target audience or have a common mission. 2. Define Mutual Benefits: Clearly articulate the benefits of the partnership for both parties. Highlight how the collaboration can help each party achieve their goals and provide clear value propositions. 3. Establish Trust and Communication: Trust is the foundation of any successful partnership. Foster open and transparent communication throughout the collaboration process and establish clear expectations from the beginning. Regularly communicate with your partners and address any concerns or challenges promptly. 4. Collaborative Problem-Solving: Foster a culture of collaboration and problem-solving. Encourage open dialogue and active participation from all partners. By working together to tackle challenges, you can build stronger relationships and find innovative solutions. 5. Create Win-Win Opportunities: Aim for mutually beneficial outcomes that create value for both your business and your partners. Explore ways to support each other's growth and success, such as cross-promotion, joint marketing initiatives, or sharing resources. 6. Regular Evaluation and Adaptation: Continuously evaluate the partnership's performance and adapt as needed. Regularly assess the partnership's effectiveness in achieving desired outcomes and make adjustments to ensure mutual success. Be open to feedback and suggestions from your partners and be willing to adapt your approach if necessary. 7. Maintain a Long-Term Perspective: Nurturing partnerships requires a long-term commitment. Prioritize building strong and enduring relationships that can withstand challenges and evolve over time. Invest time and effort in maintaining and strengthening your partnerships, even as your business grows and evolves.

# CONCLUSION

Nurturing partnerships and collaborations can fuel the growth and success of your no code SAAS business. By strategically selecting partners, establishing trust and effective communication, and fostering a collaborative mindset, you can unlock new opportunities, expand your market reach, and drive innovation. Remember to continuously evaluate and adapt your partnerships to ensure they remain mutually beneficial and aligned with your business goals.

# Chapter 36: Building SAAS for Niche Markets

When it comes to building a successful SAAS application, targeting niche markets can be a strategic approach that leads to long-term success. Niche markets are specialized segments with specific needs and requirements that are not effectively addressed by broad, generalized solutions. By focusing on a niche market, you can create a SAAS application that caters to the unique demands of a particular industry or user group. This chapter will explore the benefits of building SAAS for niche markets and provide guidance on how to effectively tap into these opportunities.

# WHY TARGET NICHE MARKETS IN SAAS?

Building a SAAS application for a niche market offers several advantages and opportunities for success: 1.

## Limited Competition:

Niche markets often have fewer competitors compared to broader markets. This means you have a higher chance of establishing yourself as a leader or dominant player within that specific market segment. 2.

## Higher Profit Margins:

As you cater to a specific target audience, you can position your SAAS application as a specialized solution. This allows you to charge premium prices and enjoy higher profit margins. 3.

## Enhanced Customer Satisfaction:

By focusing on a niche market, you can deeply understand the specific pain points and challenges faced by your target audience. This enables you to develop a tailored solution that truly meets their needs, leading to higher customer satisfaction and loyalty. 4.

# Word-of-Mouth Marketing:

Niche markets often have close-knit communities where word-of-mouth recommendations play a significant role. If your SAAS application delivers exceptional value and solves the unique problems of your target audience, satisfied customers are likely to recommend it to others within the niche, leading to organic growth and customer acquisition. 5.

# Opportunity for Expansion:

Once you establish a stronghold in a particular niche market, you can leverage your success to expand into adjacent markets or verticals. Your established expertise and credibility within the niche can give you a competitive advantage when entering new markets.

## IDENTIFYING YOUR NICHE MARKET

To successfully build a SAAS application for a niche market, it is essential to identify the right target audience. Here are some steps to help you identify your niche market: 1.

# Market Research:

Conduct thorough market research to identify industries or user groups with specific pain points and needs that are not adequately addressed by existing solutions. Look for underserved markets or segments that are willing to pay for a specialized solution. 2.

# Customer Persona Development:

Create detailed customer personas to understand the demographics, psychographics, and behavior patterns of your target audience. This will help you gain insights into their pain points, aspirations, and motivations. 3.

# Competitive Analysis:

Evaluate the competition within your target niche market. Identify existing SAAS solutions and assess their strengths, weaknesses, and gaps. This will provide insights into areas where you can innovate and differentiate your solution. 4.

# Validation:

Validate your niche market by engaging with potential customers and gathering feedback. Conduct surveys, interviews, or other forms of market testing to ensure that your solution aligns with their needs. This will help you refine your value proposition and ensure product-market fit. 5.

# Scalability:

Consider the scalability and growth potential of your chosen niche market. While focusing on a niche is beneficial, ensure that there is enough demand and room for growth in the long run.

# TAILORING YOUR SAAS APPLICATION TO THE NICHE MARKET

Once you have identified your niche market, it is important to tailor your SAAS application to address the specific needs of your target audience. Here are some strategies to consider: 1.

## Customization and Personalization:

Allow users to customize the application to fit their unique workflows and requirements. Provide options for personalization, such as branding, interface customization, and specific feature configurations. 2.

## Industry-specific Features:

Develop features and functionalities that are tailored to the specific industry or user group in your niche market. This may involve integrations with industry-specific tools, data import/export capabilities, or specialized reporting and analytics functionalities. 3.

# Domain Expertise:

Build a team with domain expertise in the niche market you are targeting. This will enable you to better understand the pain points and develop solutions that resonate with your target audience. 4.

# Seamless Integration:

Ensure that your SAAS application integrates easily with existing tools and systems commonly used within your niche market. This will enhance the overall user experience and make your solution more valuable to customers. 5.

# Continuous Feedback Loop:

Establish a feedback loop with your customers to gather insights on their evolving needs and challenges. Use this feedback to drive continuous improvement and innovation within your SAAS application.

## CONCLUSION

Building a SAAS application for a niche market can be a highly rewarding endeavor. By targeting a specific audience with specialized needs, you can differentiate yourself from competitors and establish a strong position within your niche. However, it is essential to conduct thorough market research, identify the right niche market, and tailor your application to address their unique requirements. With the right approach and execution, building a SAAS application for a niche market can lead to long-term success and financial growth.

# Chapter 37: Overcoming Imposter Syndrome in the SAAS Industry

Imposter syndrome is a phenomenon that affects many individuals in the SAAS industry. It is the persistent feeling of inadequacy or the fear of being exposed as a fraud, despite evidence of competence and accomplishments. This chapter will explore the concept of imposter syndrome in the SAAS industry and provide strategies for overcoming it.

## UNDERSTANDING IMPOSTER SYNDROME

Imposter syndrome is a psychological pattern in which individuals doubt their skills, knowledge, or accomplishments and have a persistent fear of being exposed as a fraud. This feeling can be particularly prevalent in the SAAS industry, where there is constant innovation, technical expertise, and high expectations for success. Common characteristics of imposter syndrome include: 1. Self-doubt: Feeling incapable of meeting expectations or feeling like a fraud. 2. Perfectionism: Setting unrealistic standards for oneself and fearing failure or mistakes. 3. Over-achievement: Feeling the need to constantly prove oneself through exceptional performance.

4. Discounting success: Minimizing or attributing success to luck or external factors. 5. Fear of failure: Avoiding new challenges or opportunities due to a fear of not measuring up. 6. Comparison: Constantly comparing oneself to others and feeling inferior.

# THE IMPACT OF IMPOSTER SYNDROME IN THE SAAS INDUSTRY

Imposter syndrome can have significant consequences for individuals in the SAAS industry. It can hinder personal growth, limit career progression, decrease job satisfaction, and contribute to burnout. Additionally, imposter syndrome can impede collaboration and innovation within teams, as individuals may hesitate to contribute their ideas or take on leadership roles.

# STRATEGIES FOR OVERCOMING IMPOSTER SYNDROME

Fortunately, there are several strategies that individuals in the SAAS industry can employ to overcome imposter syndrome: 1. Recognize and acknowledge your accomplishments: Take time to reflect on your achievements, skills, and experiences. Write them down and remind yourself of your capabilities and strengths. 2. Embrace failure as a learning opportunity: Recognize that failure is a natural part of the learning process and an opportunity for growth. Reframe failures as lessons rather than personal shortcomings. 3. Seek support and feedback: Reach out to mentors, colleagues, or friends who can provide guidance and support. Discuss your feelings of self-doubt and imposter syndrome with them, and ask for feedback on your accomplishments and abilities. 4. Challenge negative thoughts: Challenge negative thoughts and beliefs by questioning their validity. Replace negative self-talk with positive affirmations and focus on your strengths and past successes. 5. Set realistic goals and expectations: Avoid setting unattainable goals or comparing yourself to others. Set realistic goals that align with your skills and abilities, and celebrate milestones along the way. 6. Practice self-compassion: Be kind to yourself and treat yourself with compassion. Recognize that everyone makes mistakes and faces challenges. Practice self-care and engage in activities that bring you joy and relaxation. 7. Continuously learn and grow: Embrace a growth mindset and view challenges as opportunities for learning and development. Seek out new experiences and challenges that push you out of your comfort zone. 8. Share your story: Share your experiences and struggles with imposter syndrome with others. By opening up about your own feelings, you can create a supportive and inclusive environment where others feel comfortable sharing their own experiences.

# CONCLUSION

Imposter syndrome is a common challenge faced by individuals in the SAAS industry. However, by recognizing and addressing imposter syndrome, it is possible to overcome self-doubt and achieve personal and professional success. By implementing strategies such as acknowledging accomplishments, seeking support, challenging negative thoughts, and practicing self-compassion, individuals can build confidence, embrace their skills, and thrive in the SAAS industry.

# Chapter 38: Earning Passive Income with No Code SAAS

Earning passive income is a goal for many individuals looking to achieve financial freedom and break free from the traditional 9-to-5 job. With the rise of no code SAAS platforms, it has become increasingly accessible for entrepreneurs to create and monetize software applications with minimal ongoing effort. In this chapter, we will explore various strategies and best practices for earning passive income with no code SAAS.

## UNDERSTANDING PASSIVE INCOME

Passive income refers to the earnings generated from an investment or business that does not require active involvement or continuous effort. It allows individuals to make money while they sleep, creating a sense of financial security and independence. The concept of passive income aligns well with the no code SAAS industry, as these platforms facilitate the creation of software applications that can generate ongoing revenue with minimal ongoing effort.

# MONETIZING YOUR NO CODE SAAS APPLICATION

To earn passive income with your no code SAAS application, it's essential to have a solid monetization strategy in place. Here are some effective approaches to consider:

## Subscription Model

Implementing a subscription-based pricing model is one of the most common and effective ways to generate passive income. With this model, users pay a recurring fee for continued access to your SAAS application. You can offer different subscription tiers with varying features and pricing to cater to different customer segments. This recurring revenue stream can provide consistent and predictable income over time.

## License Fees

If your no code SAAS application offers a unique and valuable solution, you can consider charging a one-time license fee for access to the software. This approach works well for niche markets or specific industries where customers are willing to pay a higher upfront cost for a perpetual license.

# Upselling and Add-Ons

Another strategy for earning passive income is to offer upsells and add-ons to your customers. Upselling involves persuading customers to upgrade to a higher-priced version of your SAAS application, while add-ons can provide additional features or services at an extra cost. These tactics can increase the average revenue per customer and generate additional income without significant ongoing effort.

# Affiliate Partnerships

Consider establishing affiliate partnerships with complementary products or services. By promoting other relevant products or services to your customer base, you can earn passive income through referral or affiliate commissions. This approach requires minimal ongoing effort once the initial integration and setup are complete.

# White Labeling and Reseller Programs

Offering white labeling options or reseller programs can be an effective way to earn passive income. This strategy involves allowing other businesses to rebrand and sell your SAAS application as their own, while you earn a percentage of the revenue generated. It allows you to leverage other businesses' networks and customer base to expand your reach and generate additional income.

# Advertising and Sponsorships

If your no code SAAS application attracts a large user base or targets a specific niche, you may consider incorporating advertising or sponsorship opportunities. This can include displaying third-party ads within your application or partnering with relevant brands for sponsored content. However, it's important to strike a balance between monetization and user experience to maintain the integrity and usability of your application.

# Marketplace Revenue

If your no code SAAS platform has a built-in marketplace where users can sell their own applications or extensions, you can earn passive income by taking a percentage of the revenue generated from those transactions. This approach leverages the community and network effect of your platform, allowing users to create and sell their own products while you earn a share of the profits.

# AUTOMATING BUSINESS OPERATIONS

To truly earn passive income with your no code SAAS application, it's crucial to automate as many business operations as possible. By streamlining processes and minimizing manual labor, you can reduce ongoing effort and focus on strategic growth and optimization. Here are some areas of your SAAS business that can be automated:

# User Onboarding and Support

Implementing automated user onboarding processes and integrating self-service support options can provide a seamless and efficient experience for your customers. Utilize chatbots or AI-powered customer support tools to handle common inquiries and escalations, freeing up your time and resources.

# Payment Processing and Invoicing

Integrate payment processing and invoicing systems into your no code SAAS application to automate the billing process. This ensures that customers are billed correctly and on time, reducing the need for manual intervention.

# Analytics and Reporting

Leverage analytics and reporting tools to automate the collection and analysis of user data. This data can provide valuable insights into customer behavior, usage patterns, and revenue generation. By automating this process, you can make data-driven decisions and optimize your SAAS application without constant manual effort.

# Marketing and Lead Generation

Implement marketing automation tools to streamline lead generation and customer acquisition processes. This can include automated email campaigns, drip campaigns, and customer segmentation based on user behavior. By nurturing leads automatically, you can continuously generate new customers without significant ongoing effort.

# Infrastructure Scaling and Maintenance

Leverage cloud infrastructure and serverless architectures to automate scaling and maintenance tasks. By utilizing platforms like AWS (Amazon Web Services) or Azure, you can automate processes such as server provisioning, monitoring, and scaling based on demand. This ensures that your SAAS application remains available and responsive without manual intervention.

## CONCLUSION

Earning passive income with no code SAAS applications is an achievable goal with the right monetization strategy and automation in place. By implementing a subscription model, upselling, utilizing affiliate partnerships, or exploring advertising opportunities, you can generate ongoing revenue without continuous manual effort. Additionally, automating various aspects of your SAAS business operations allows you to allocate your time and resources towards growth and innovation, facilitating the journey towards financial independence and success as a no code SAAS entrepreneur.Investing in No Code SAAS Startups is an exciting opportunity for individuals looking to capitalize on the growing trend of no code development and the thriving software-as-a-service (SAAS) industry. This chapter explores the potential benefits and considerations of investing in these startups, as well as strategies for making smart investment decisions. Investing in No Code SAAS Startups offers numerous advantages for both investors and entrepreneurs. From the investor's perspective, it provides an opportunity to generate significant returns on investment, as successful startups in the SAAS space have achieved impressive valuations and growth rates. Additionally, investing in no code SAAS startups allows investors to diversify their portfolios and participate in an industry that is projected to continue expanding in the coming years. For entrepreneurs, securing funding from investors is crucial for scaling their businesses and achieving their growth objectives. No code SAAS startups often require capital for development, marketing, customer acquisition, and expansion. By investing in these startups, investors provide the necessary resources for entrepreneurs to realize their vision and build successful SAAS applications. When considering investing in No Code SAAS Startups, there are several key factors to evaluate. Firstly, it is important to assess the market potential and demand for the SAAS application. Conducting thorough market research and analyzing industry trends can help investors determine the viability and scalability of the startup. Additionally, understanding the competitive landscape and identifying the startup's unique value proposition is essential for assessing its potential for success. Investors should also consider the experience and track record of the entrepreneurial team behind the startup. A strong and capable team with relevant expertise can significantly impact the chances of success. Assessing their past achievements, industry knowledge, and ability to execute on their business plan can provide valuable insights into the startup's potential for growth. Furthermore, examining the financials of the startup, including revenue projections, cost structure, and profitability, is crucial for making informed investment decisions. Investors should carefully review the startup's business model, pricing strategy, and monetization plans to ensure they align with industry standards and have the potential for generating sustainable revenue. In terms of investment strategies, investors can choose to invest directly in early-stage no code SAAS startups or participate in funding rounds through venture capital firms or angel investor networks. Direct investment allows for more hands-on involvement, while investing through established firms provides access to a curated portfolio of startups and professional due diligence. As with any investment, it is important to conduct thorough due diligence and consider the risks involved. Investing in startups inherently carries risks, including the potential for failure, market volatility, and the lack of liquidity. Diversifying one's investment portfolio and seeking professional advice can help mitigate these risks and increase the chances of a successful investment. In conclusion, investing in No Code SAAS Startups presents an exciting opportunity for individuals to participate in the rapidly growing SAAS industry. By carefully evaluating market potential, entrepreneurial teams, financials, and investment strategies, investors can make informed decisions and potentially achieve significant financial returns. Investing in no code SAAS startups not only supports entrepreneurship and innovation but also provides a pathway to participate in a thriving industry that is transforming the way software applications are developed and deployed.

# Chapter 40: Becoming a Millionaire with No Code SAAS Applications

Becoming a millionaire in the software-as-a-service (SAAS) industry is an achievable goal with the rise of no code SAAS applications. With the right strategies and execution, you can create a successful SAAS business and achieve financial success. In this chapter, we will explore the key steps and considerations to become a millionaire with no code SAAS applications.

## IDENTIFY A PROBLEM AND MARKET DEMAND

The first step towards becoming a millionaire with a no code SAAS application is to identify a problem that needs solving in the market. Conduct thorough market research to understand the pain points and challenges faced by potential customers. Look for gaps and opportunities where a SAAS solution can provide value and address these problems.

# CREATE A COMPELLING VALUE PROPOSITION

Once you have identified the problem, develop a compelling value proposition that clearly communicates the unique benefits and advantages your SAAS application offers. Highlight how it solves the pain points of your target audience and differentiates itself from competitors. A strong value proposition will attract customers and set the foundation for your path to success.

# BUILD A USER-FRIENDLY AND INTUITIVE SAAS APPLICATION

Invest time and effort into building a user-friendly and intuitive SAAS application. No code platforms provide the tools and functionalities to create visually appealing and easy-to-use interfaces. Pay attention to the user experience (UX) and ensure that your application is intuitive and meets the needs of your target audience. A seamless user experience will increase customer satisfaction and drive growth.

# IMPLEMENT EFFECTIVE MONETIZATION STRATEGIES

To become a millionaire with your no code SAAS application, implementing effective monetization strategies is vital. Consider various pricing models, such as subscription-based pricing, usage-based pricing, freemium models, or one-time purchase options. Additionally, explore other revenue streams like add-ons, upsells, partner programs, and reseller agreements. Experiment with different approaches to find the right balance between generating revenue and providing value to your customers.

# EXECUTE A COMPREHENSIVE MARKETING STRATEGY

A well-executed marketing strategy is crucial for reaching a broader audience and driving user acquisition. Develop a comprehensive marketing plan that includes various channels, such as content marketing, social media marketing, influencer marketing, search engine optimization (SEO), and referral programs. Clearly communicate the value of your SAAS application, engage with your target audience, and continuously refine your marketing efforts based on feedback and data analysis.

# FOCUS ON CUSTOMER SUCCESS AND RETENTION

To achieve long-term success and become a millionaire with your no code SAAS application, prioritize customer success and retention. Provide exceptional customer support, regularly update and enhance your application based on user feedback, personalize the user experience, and implement loyalty programs or rewards to encourage customer loyalty. Satisfied and loyal customers not only contribute to steady revenue but also act as advocates for your SAAS application.

# CONTINUOUSLY INNOVATE AND SCALE

Innovation and scaling are key factors in becoming a millionaire with your no code SAAS application. Continuously innovate and stay ahead of the competition by researching industry trends, collaborating with users and stakeholders, staying agile, embracing emerging technologies, and investing in research and development. As your SAAS application gains traction, focus on scaling by expanding your user base, streamlining operations, and exploring new markets or opportunities.

# STAY RESILIENT AND PERSIST

The road to becoming a millionaire in the SAAS industry is not without challenges. Stay resilient and persistent in pursuing your goals. Embrace failures as learning opportunities, constantly adapt and improve your strategies, and maintain a positive mindset. Building a successful SAAS business takes time and effort, but with perseverance, you can attain the financial success you desire.

# Conclusion

Becoming a millionaire with no code SAAS applications is an achievable goal for entrepreneurs who are willing to put in the work and execute the right strategies. Identify a problem, create a compelling value proposition, build a user-friendly application, implement effective monetization strategies, execute a comprehensive marketing plan, focus on customer success and retention, continuously innovate and scale, and maintain resilience and persistence. By following these steps, you can pave the way to becoming a millionaire in the thriving SAAS industry.

www.ingramcontent.com/pod-product-compliance
Lightning Source LLC
Chambersburg PA
CBHW050447290526
45786CB00006B/2195